'World's moving. People moving. We've only to cross the sea. Same sea we're looking at. The world's waiting for us. We've only to take our place in it.'

A rich, epic work, *Victoria* comprises three separate but interweaving plays. In 1936, 1974 and 1996 a woman is witness to the shifting political and social history of Britain in the twentieth century, her life shaped by dramatic events in a rural community on the Scottish coast.

Joyous, erotic and poetic, *Victoria* stands firmly in the long tradition of RSC playwriting.

David Greig was born in Edinburgh and currently lives and works in Scotland. His plays have been extensively staged in Britain and Europe. His previous work includes *The Speculator* (1999, Edinburgh International Festival/Grec Festival, Barcelona), *The cosmonaut's last message to the woman he once loved in the former Soviet Union* (1999, Paines Plough, tour, Tron Theatre, Glasgow), *Danny 306 +me 4ever* (1999, Traverse Theatre, Edinburgh), *Caledonia Dreaming* (1997, 7:84 Theatre Company, Scotland), *The Architect* (1996, Traverse Theatre) and *Europe* (1995, Traverse Theatre). In 1990 he co-founded Suspect Culture, an international theatre company based in Glasgow. For Suspect Culture he has collaborated in the creation of, and written, *Candide 2000* (2000, Scottish Tour), *Mainstream* (1999, international tour), *Timeless* (1997, Edinburgh International Festival), *Airport* (1996 and 1998 international tour) and *One Way Street* (1994, international tour). He is currently dramaturg for the company. Outside the theatre, his writing includes the films *Schiehallion* (BBC Scotland) and *Nightlife* (BBC Scotland) and the radio plays *The Swansong* (BBC Radio 4) and *Copper Sulphate* (BBC Radio 3).

Published by Methuen 2000

1 3 5 7 9 10 8 6 4 2

First published in the Great Britain in 2000 by Methuen Publishing Limited
215 Vauxhall Bridge Road, London SW1V 1EJ

Copyright © 2000 David Greig

The author has asserted his rights under the Copyright, Designs and
Patents Act, 1988, to be identified as the author of this work

Methuen Publishing Limited Reg. No. 3543167

A CIP catalogue record is available from the British Library

ISBN 0 413 75090 6

Typeset by SX Composing DTP, Rayleigh, Essex
Printed and bound in Great Britain by
Cox & Wyman Ltd, Reading, Berkshire

Victoria

David Greig

Methuen

THE ROYAL SHAKESPEARE COMPANY

The Royal Shakespeare Company is probably one of the best-known theatre companies in the world. It has operated in its present form since 1961, when it changed its name from the Shakespeare Memorial Theatre Company, established a London base and widened its repertoire to embrace works other than Shakespeare.

Today the RSC has five home theatres. In Stratford the Royal Shakespeare Theatre stages large-scale productions of Shakespeare's plays; the Swan, a galleried Jacobean playhouse, brings to light the plays of many of his neglected contemporaries alongside classics of world theatre, while The Other Place, the company's studio theatre, houses some of the company's most exciting experimental and contemporary work, as well as providing a regular venue for visiting companies and some of the RSC's education work, including the annual Prince of Wales Shakespeare School.

In 1982 the company moved its London home to the Barbican Centre, where in the large-scale Barbican Theatre and the studio-sized Pit, the company stages work transferring from Stratford as well as new productions.

But Stratford and London are only part of the story. Recent years have seen a dramatic increase in the reach of the RSC, with major RSC productions on tour around the UK and abroad, in addition to the company's annual resident seasons in Newcastle upon Tyne and Plymouth. Productions from Stratford and London visit regional theatres, while our annual regional tour continues to set up its own travelling auditorium in schools and community centres around the country. This ensures that the RSC's productions are available to the widest possible number of people geographically. A lively programme of education work accompanies all this, creating the audiences of tomorrow by bringing the excitement and the power of theatre to young people all over the country.

International touring has always been part of the RSC's agenda, and in the past few years the company has taken Shakespeare to enthusiastic audiences in Europe, the USA, Australia, New Zealand, South America, Japan, India and Pakistan. This year the company will also visit Hong Kong, Spain, Turkey and Korea. The RSC is grateful to The British Council for its support of its overseas touring programme.

Despite enormous changes over the years, the company today is still formed around a core of associate actors and actresses, whose artistic talents combine with those of the world's top directors and designers and the most highly-skilled technical workshops to give a distinctive and unmistakable approach to theatre. The play you are seeing tonight is at once a link in a great tradition and a unique event.

THE ROYAL SHAKESPEARE COMPANY

RSC EDUCATION

The objective of the RSC Education Department is to enable as many people as possible from all walks of life to have easy access to the great works of Shakespeare, the Renaissance and the Theatre.

To do this, we are building a team which supports the productions that the company presents onstage for the general public, special interest groups and education establishments of all kinds.

We are also planning to develop our contribution as a significant learning resource in the fields of Shakespeare, the Renaissance, classical and modern theatre, theatre arts and the RSC. This resource is made available in many different ways, including workshops, teachers' programmes, summer courses, a menu of activities offered to group members of the audience, pre- and post-show events as part of the Events programme, open days, tours of the theatre, community activities, youth programmes, loans of parts of the RSC Collection for exhibitions etc.

We are building, for use world wide, a new web site to be launched this year. This will make available all of the above, as well as providing access to the RSC's collection of historic theatre and Shakespearean material. It will also carry interesting and interactive material about the work of the RSC.

We can also use our knowledge of theatre techniques to help in other aspects of learning: classroom teaching techniques for subjects other than drama or English, including management and personnel issues.

Not all of these programmes are available all the time, and not all of them are yet in place. However, if you are interested in pursuing any of these options, the telephone numbers and e-mail addresses are as follows:

For information on general education activities, contact Education Administrator Sarah Keevill on 01789 403462, or e-mail her on sarah.keevill@rsc.org.uk.

To find out about backstage tours, please contact our Tour Manager Anne Tippett on 01789 403405, or e-mail her on theatre.tours@rsc.org.uk.

JOIN THE RSC

For £8 a year you can join the RSC's Mailing List as an Associate member. Regular mailings will bring you:

* Advance Information and priority booking for RSC seasons in Stratford, London, Newcastle and Plymouth

* Deferred payment facilities for the London Season and the Stratford Summer Festival Season 2000 when tickets are paid for by credit card

* Seasonal offers on the Stratford StopOver scheme

* Special members' events in Stratford and London

* Details of UK and overseas touring and information about RSC transfers to the West End.

* Free RSC Magazine

* No fees payable on ticket re-sales in Stratford.

* Full membership at £24, social groups at £10 and education groups at £8 give even more benefits

Overseas Members. The RSC tours regularly overseas. Wherever you are in the world, you can be a member of the RSC's mailing List. Overseas Membership is available from £15.

STAY IN TOUCH

For up-to-date news on the RSC, our productions and education work, visit the RSC's official web site: **www.rsc.org.uk**. Further information on the RSC is also available on Teletext.

A PARTNERSHIP WITH THE RSC

The RSC is immensely grateful for the valuable support of its corporate sponsors and individual and charitable donors. Between them these groups provide over £6m a year for the RSC and support a range of initiatives such as actor training, education workshops and access to our performances for all members of society.

Amongst our corporate sponsors, we are especially grateful to Allied Domecq, principal sponsor since 1994, for its far-sighted and long-standing relationship. Allied Domecq's announcement that its principal sponsorship will come to a natural end in 2001 provides an exciting opportunity for companies to form new corporate partnerships with the RSC, as principal sponsor, as a member of the RSC's new Business Partners programme or as a corporate member.

As an individual you may wish to support the work of the RSC through membership of the RSC Patrons. For as little as £21 per month you can join a cast drawn from our audience and the worlds of theatre, film, politics and business. Alternatively, the gift of a legacy to the RSC would enable the Company to maintain and increase new artistic and educational work with children and adults through the Acting and Education Funds.

For information about corporate partnership with the RSC,
please contact Robert Fleming
Head of Sponsorship Development
Barbican Theatre, London EC2Y 8BQ
Tel: 020 7382 7139
E-mail: robert.fleming@rsc.org.uk

For information about individual relationships with the RSC,
please contact Graeme Williamson
Development Manager
Royal Shakespeare Theatre, Waterside
Stratford-upon-Avon CV37 6BB
Tel: 01789 412661
E-mail: graemew@rsc.org.uk
You can visit our web site at www.rsc.org.uk/development

SOME BACKGROUND MATERIAL

The Highlands

The thing which impresses most about the wild scenery in this part of the highlands is its strangeness. Geologists give the explanation that the mountains here consist of two formations which have piled up in confusion so that the summits belonging to one of them sometimes burst through the surface of the other. One's actual impression of these peaks is that they do not belong to this world as we know it at all, but to a much older one; I had this feeling before I knew the geological explanation of it.

EDWIN MUIR, *SCOTTISH JOURNEY* (1935)

O great Island, Island of my love,
many a night of them I fancied
the great ocean itself restless
agitated with love of you
as you lay on the sea,
you beautiful bird of Scotland,
your supremely beautiful wings bent
about many-nooked Lake Bracadale,
your beautiful wings prostrate on the sea
from the Wild Stallion to the Aird of Sleat,
your joyous wings spread
about Loch Snizort and the world.
...

Great Island, Island of my desire,
Island of my heart and wound,
it is not likely that the strife
and suffering of Braes will be seen requited
and it is not certain that the debts
of the Glendale Martyr will be made good,
there is no hope of your townships
rising high with gladness and laughter,
and your men are not expected
when America and France take them.

Pity the eye that sees on the ocean
the great dead bird of Scotland.

SORLEY MACLEAN, FROM 'THE ISLAND'

The concept of the 'Highlands' does not appear in the written evidence for the period before 1400 despite the geographical division between the north and the south of Scotland. When the Highlands did become part of the vocabulary in the medieval period, it was in response to a need to isolate and distinguish a part of Scotland that differed in cultural and social terms from the rest. A crucial difference was linguistic for, as Gaelic retreated from the Lowlands, the 'Highlands' became more culturally distinctive and linguistically separate from other parts of the kingdom. Very quickly, too, it became regarded by the state as a problem region. In the early modern period, Highland instability was seen as a major obstacle to the effective unification of the country. After the Reformation, the Highlands were not properly evangelised for the new faith and were regarded as irreligious, popish and pagan for generations thereafter. For the Scottish political élites and the Presbyterian Church before 1700, the Highlands were alien and hostile, in need of greater state control and both moral and religious 'improvement'....In the later eighteenth century the land ceased to be regarded as simply repellent and came to be viewed as beautiful, romantic and inspiring. Modern notions of 'scenery' and scenic beauty were born and resulted in a transformation of aesthetic responses to the Highlands....These new ideas helped to transform the perception of the Highlands from a barren wilderness to a place of compelling natural beauty.

T M DEVINE, *THE SCOTTISH NATION 1700-2000* (1999)

What Highlands communities have at their best...
is stability, courage, kindness and a sense of
belonging together, of being able to call on one
another in times of stress....There was considerable
oppression [historically], and where there was not,
there was still a big social gap, as in rural England,
between the Big House and the rest. This society,
inaccurately called feudal, did mean a closer,
warmer bond between the poor. The Big House
might be lonely. The poor were not....One must
also, however, remember the Highland depressive
condition, caused by many things, a population
pyramid over-weighted at the elderly end, a
repressive form of Protestantism, two centuries of
oppression from above, and a feeling of inferiority
and helplessness, typically colonial, and partly
due to an educational system which has for many
generations downgraded Highland language and
culture.

NAOMI MITCHINSON, *OIL FOR THE HIGHLANDS?* (1974)

The Highlands have had a political influence
on Scotland, and indeed on London, far out of
proportion to the size of their population, during
most of their remembered history. From the
fourteenth century when the Lords of the Isles
ruled half Scotland, virtually a state within a state,
and treated directly with the English kings; to the
Clearances of the nineteenth century, when lurid
stories of crofters burnt out of their cottages
sowed seeds of a guilt complex which exists to
the present day, the Highlands have been a source
of irritation and frustration for central governments
down the ages. But they have also been the focus
for enormous efforts by governments and their
agencies to inject new life into a rural economy
which has been in a state of decline for as long
as anyone can remember.

TORCUIL CRICHTON IN *ANATOMY OF SCOTLAND* (1992)

The 1930s

Never has such turmoil
nor vehement trouble been put in my flesh
by Christ's suffering on the earth
or by the millions of the skies.

And I took of heed of a vapid dream -
green wood of the land of story -
as when my stubborn heart leaped to the glint
of her smile and golden head.

And her beauty cast a cloud
over poverty and a bitter wound
and over the world of Lenin's intellect,
over his patience and his anger.

SORLEY MACLEAN, 'THE TURMOIL' (1943)

Throughout the 1930s I was obsessed with
politics. I remember as a boy at school in 1926,
away up in Portree, being completely in favour
of the General Strike, and of the miners' struggle
after it collapsed. The Great Depression and the
likelihood that all Europe would soon be Fascist
made me passionately political, and what poetry I
wrote was full of conflict. Much of it was a quarrel
with myself for my lack of single-mindedness,
which made my verse confessional rather than
propagandist. Family reasons kept me from Spain
in 1936-37, but in my heart of hearts I knew then
that I 'preferred a woman to crescent history',
and was frank about it.

SORLEY MACLEAN, *COLLECTED POEMS* (1989)

The exact number of British volunteers is not
known; in the early days some arrived in Spain
unrecorded, while during the war the continuous
fighting made precise documentation impossible.
The records of those who went through London to

the fighting unit contain 2,010 names...By the time
the British Battalion was formed early in 1937, the
overwhelming majority of the volunteers were
industrial workers...From Scotland came 437...

BILL ALEXANDER, *BRITISH VOLUNTEERS FOR LIBERTY* (1982)

Coming, in September, through the thin streets,
I thought back to another year I knew,
Autumn, lifting potatoes and stacking peats
On Mull, while the Atlantic's murky blue
Swung sluggishly in past Jura, and the hills
Were brown lions, crouched to meet the autumn gales.

In the hard rain and the rip of thunder,
I remembered the haze coming in from the sea
And the clatter of Gaelic voices by the breakwater
Or in the fields as the reapers took their tea;
I remembered the foal lying where it died,
Which we buried, one evening, above high-tide
...

In September, I saw the drab newspapers
Telling of wars, in Spain and in the East,
And wished I'd stayed on Mull, their gestures
Frightened me and made me feel the unwanted guest,
The burden on the house who having taken salt
Cannot be ejected, however grave his fault.

In September, we lit the fire and talked together,
Discussing the trivialities of a spent day
And what we would eat. I forgot the weather
And the dull streets and the sun on Islay,
And all my fear. I lost my carefully-kept count
Of the tides to death, and, in September, was
content.

RUTHVEN TODD, FROM 'IN SEPTEMBER' (1937)

It was the first time I had ever been in a town
where the working-class was in the saddle.
Practically every building of any size had been
seized by the workers and had been draped with
red flags or with the red and black flag of the
Anarchists; every wall was scrawled with the
hammer and sickle and with the initials of the
revolutionary parties; almost every church had
been gutted and its images burnt....Every shop
and café had an inscription saying that it had
been collectivised; even the bootblacks had
been collectivised and their boxes painted red
and black. Waiters and shop-walkers looked you
in the face and treated you as an equal....Tipping
was forbidden by law....There was much in it I did
not understand, in some ways I did not even like it,
but I recognised it immediately as a state of affairs
worth fighting for.

GEORGE ORWELL, *HOMAGE TO CATALONIA* (1938)

Next to my own skin, her pearls. My mistress
bids me wear them, warm them, until evening
when I'll brush her hair. At six, I place them
round her cool, white throat. All day I think of her,
resting in the Yellow Room, contemplating silk
or taffeta, which gown tonight? She fans herself
whilst I work willingly, my slow heat entering
each pearl. Slack on my neck, her rope.

She's beautiful. I dream about her
in my attic bed; picture her dancing
with tall men, puzzled by my faint, persistent scent
beneath her French perfume, her milky stones.

I dust her shoulders with a rabbit's foot,
watch the soft blush seep through her skin
like an indolent sigh. In her looking-glass
my red lips part as though I want to speak.

Full moon. Her carriage brings her home. I see
her every movement in my head...Undressing,
taking off her jewels, her slim hand reaching
for the case, slipping naked into bed, the way

she always does...And I lie here awake,
knowing the pearls are cooling even now
in the room where my mistress sleeps. All night
I feel their absence and I burn.

CAROL ANN DUFFY, 'WARMING HER PEARLS' (1987)

It is tempting to paint the experience of women
in the inter-war period in dark colours. By the
standards of the later twentieth century they
did face discrimination and inequality based on
gender differences. But women at the time did not
see their lives in such negative terms. For young
girls in work, this was a period of rising incomes
and more opportunity to spend on such pastimes
as the cinema and dancing. Some might see
women 'ghetto-ised' in the home and in poorly
paid jobs, but oral evidence suggests that groups
as varied as domestic servants, shop assistants,
seamstresses, teachers and nurses derived
considerable satisfaction and pride from their
work. Most crucially, the same sources, and
notably the Stirling women's history project, reveal
the pivotal status and importance of wives and
mothers in the family who may not have carried
out paid employment but who had a demanding
and fulfilling responsibility in bringing up several
children, keeping their homes clean and tidy and
managing tight household budgets.

T M DEVINE, *THE SCOTTISH NATION 1700-2000* (1999)

Savitri Devi was a Frenchwoman of Greek-English
birth who had become an admirer of German
National Socialism in the late 1920s and was
obsessed by the Aryan myth. Deeply impressed
by its racial heritage and caste system, she had
emigrated to India in the early 1930s to acquaint
herself at first hand with what she regarded as the
cradle of the Aryan race....Savitri Devi elaborated
an extraordinary synthesis of Hindu religion and

Nordic racial ideology involving the polar origin
of the Aryans, the cycle of the ages, and the
incarnation of the last avatar of Vishnu in Adolf
Hitler. She regarded the Third Reich as 'the holy
Land of the West, the Stronghold of regenerate
Aryanism.'...[She also wrote:] 'If those of Indo-
European race regard the conquest of pagan
Europe by Christianity as a decadence, then
the whole of Hindu India can be likened to a last
fortress of very ancient ideals, of very old and
beautiful religious and metaphysical conceptions,
which have already passed away in Europe.
Hinduism is thus the last flourishing and fecund
branch on an immense tree which has been cut
down and mutilated for two thousand years.'...
She dismissed Christianity and other creedal
religions for their exclusive concentration on man:
'[T]heir centre of interest is man, the background,
man's short history, man's misery, man's craving
for happiness; the scope, man's salvation.' In
Hinduism this anthropocentric view had no place.
The center of interest was the external universe of
existence, in which man was only a detail.

NICHOLAS GOODRICK-CLARKE, *HITLER'S PRIESTESS* (1998)

The 1970s

The SNP argued that there was a way out of the
spiral of decline if an independent Scotland took
control of the enormous oil resources now
becoming available in the North Sea. In October
1970, BP struck oil 110 miles off Aberdeen in
what was to become the giant Forties field. The
inflation in world oil prices after the Arab-Israeli
War meant that even marginal fields could have
huge potential value. Recovery of the 'black gold'
and expansion in the area of exploration proceeded
apace. The SNP oil campaign began in 1971 and
brilliantly exploited the contrast between, on the
one hand, the fabulous wealth found off Scotland's

coasts and, on the other, the fact that by then the Scots had the worst unemployment rate in western Europe and were yoked to a British state that stumbled from crisis to crisis. Oil also gave the nationalist argument a new credibility by demonstrating that an independent Scotland might indeed survive out of its own resources.

T M DEVINE, *THE SCOTTISH NATION 1700-2000* (1999)

As a political slogan, 'It's Scotland's Oil', the Nationalist battle-cry of the 1970s, spoke with greater resonance than meaning. In the legal, constitutional and fiscal senses, it was not Scotland's oil. The revenues, totalling some £80 billion since the first oil came ashore in 1975, have been paid into the British, not a Scottish, Exchequer, and used to Scotland's benefit only in accordance with the normal dispensations of public expenditure policy. Their principal use has been to underwrite the economic reconstruction of the United Kingdom which the Thatcher Government, whose election in 1979 coincided with the first great surge of North Sea production... felt to be opportune and necessary....But its impact on the Scottish economy has been, and remains, profound. Scotland may not have had the revenue, but it has enjoyed substantial gain, including employment. In mid-1990, according to an SDA/Training Agency/ Scottish Office survey, one in two hundred Scottish jobs was directly related to the oil industry...

KEITH AITKEN IN *ANATOMY OF SCOTLAND* (1992)

We have curious feelings of pride and guilt about the Highlands; perhaps we should stop and think what these are all about....But may the pride not be grounded in knowledge that there is something about the Highlands which may be missing

elsewhere but is an essential element in human society which is in danger in most places and which we eliminate at our peril? Is the increasing inroad of the money standard for everything going to destroy something in the Highlands which though elusive is very important?...The Highlands may still have an alternative in which people can live in a fully human, non-centralised way.

NAOMI MITCHINSON, *OIL FOR THE HIGHLANDS?* (1974)

The 1990s

Today, no geographical region of Britain has more agencies to administer it and to speak on its behalf than the Highlands. But whether there is any real political or economic power left in the area itself is open to question. The most basic resources, the land and the sea, remain firmly outwith the control of the people who live there, with fiscal and economic power exerted from further south.

TORCUIL CRICHTON IN *ANATOMY OF SCOTLAND* (1992)

Scotland faces a crisis of identity and survival. It is now being governed without consent and subject to the declared intention of having imposed upon it a radical change of outlook and behaviour pattern which it shows no sign of wanting. All questions as to whether consent should be a part of government are brushed aside. The comments of Adam Smith are put to uses which would have astonished him, Scottish history is selectively distorted and the Scots are told that their votes are lying; that they secretly love what they constantly vote against....Scotland, if it is to remain Scotland, can no longer live with such a constitution and has nothing to hope from it.

CAMPAIGN FOR A SCOTTISH ASSEMBLY, *A CLAIM OF RIGHT FOR SCOTLAND* (1988)

The station is in the middle of a moor. There appears to be no habitation around. In the distance are some hills.

TOMMY: It's the great outdoors.... It's fresh air.... Doesn't it make you proud to be Scottish?

RENTON: I hate being Scottish. We're the lowest of the fucking low, the scum of the earth, the most wretched, servile, miserable, pathetic trash that was ever shat into civilisation. Some people hate the English, but I don't. They're just wankers. We, on the other hand, are colonised by wankers. We can't even pick a decent culture to be colonised by. We are ruled by effete arseholes. It's a shite state of affairs and all the fresh air in the world will not make any fucking difference.

JOHN HODGE, *TRAINSPOTTING* (SCREENPLAY, 1996, FROM THE NOVEL BY IRVINE WELSH)

[After the 1992 General Election] Vision was out of fashion; party sectarianism oozed back into the daylight; and boldness seemed discredited as mere ranting vanity. Many of the amateur politicians noted the cynicism of the professionals and turned back to their golf handicaps and the rosebeds. Scotland seemed, yet again, to have confirmed the judgement of the poet Edwin Muir in the 1930s:

This is a difficult land. Here things miscarry
Whether we care or do not care enough...

Yet again the Scottish political world had slithered from delusion to disillusion - it had accomplished its familiar waterslide into cold porridge.

ANDREW MARR, *THE BATTLE FOR SCOTLAND* (1992)

On the civic amenity landfill site,
the coup, the dump beyond the cemetery
and the 30-mile-an-hour sign, her stiff
old ladies' bags, open mouthed, spew
postcards sent from small Scots towns
in 1960: Peebles, Largs, the rock-gardens
of Carnoustie, tinted in the dirt.
Mr and Mrs Scotland, here is the hand you were dealt:
fair but cool, showery but nevertheless,
Jean asks kindly; the lovely scenery;
in careful school-room script -
The Beltane Queen was crowned today
But Mr and Mrs Scotland are dead.

Couldn't he have burned them? Released
in a grey curl of smoke
this pattern for a cable knit? Or this:
tossed between a toppled fridge
and sweet-stinking anorak: *Dictionary for Mothers*
M: - Milk, *the woman who worries* ... ;
And here, Mr Scotland's John Bull Puncture Repair Kit;
those days when he knew intimately
the thin roads of his country, hedgerows
hanged with small black brambles' heats;
and here, for God's sake his last few joiner's tools,
SCOTLAND, SCOTLAND, stamped on their tired
handles.

Do we take them? Before the bulldozer comes
to make more room, to shove aside
his shaving brush, her button tin.
Do we save this toolbox, these old-fashioned views
addressed, after all, to Mr and Mrs Scotland?
Should we reach and take them? And then?
Forget them, till that person enters
our silent house, begins to open
to the light our kitchen drawers,
and performs for us this perfunctory rite:
the sweeping up, the turning out.

KATHLEEN JAMIE, 'MR AND MRS SCOTLAND' (1994)

Savitri Devi's influence on international neo-Fascism and other hybrid strains of mystical fascism has been continuous since the 1960s and beyond her death [in 1982] into the 1990s. But the very eccentricity of her thought, combining as it does Aryan supremacism and anti-Semitism with Hinduism, animal rights, and a fundamentally biocentric view of life, has led to strange alliances in radical ideology....In [Neo-fascist] writings paganism, magic, the natural order act as a foil for a cleansing wave of fascist violence that will sweep away a corrupt humanity, leaving only Aryans in possession of a pristine world. Their thought is undeniably fascist in inspiration, but her ideas also hold an appeal for 'alternative' movements whose inspiration is far removed from such sources....With the advent of the New Age movement, man was felt to have lost his roots in nature, leading an artificial life among machines and automated processes that robbed him of his humanity and a meaningful life....Green thinkers are especially pessimistic about the effects of human population on nature. An extreme school of ecological catastrophism regards all human civilisation as deleterious and evil....Deep Ecology, biocentrism, nature worship, and New Age paganism reflect a hostility towards Christianity, rationalism, and liberalism in modern society. Although these radical movements often have their roots in left-wing dissent, their increasing tendency toward myth and despair indicate their susceptibility to millenarian and mystical ideas on the far right. Neo-Nazi and fascist activities now actively seek to infiltrate the ecological and esoteric scene.

NICHOLAS GOODRICK-CLARKE, *HITLER'S PRIESTESS* (1998)

Piper Alpha, 6 July 1988; Lockerbie, 21 December 1988; Dunblane, 13 March 1996: if Europe and the rest of the world encountered Scotland it was through these catastrophes and not through economic adaptation, the autonomy movement of cultural revival. The three disasters were not, however, acts of God. The Piper Alpha platform, as Lord Cullen's inquiry established in 1990, was overloaded and ill-maintained, through pressure to maximise oil and gas output. Those responsible for the Lockerbie bombing are shadowy: Arab terrorists, drug dealers, secret service spooks? The killing of the Dunblane children exposed both the availability of lethal handguns and the way in which other 'close-knit communities' had trusted their children to a disturbed and dangerous misfit, rather than undertake voluntary activities themselves.

No-one was an island, and globally there was much to be pessimistic about. A warmer climate aided Scots tourism, but the thinning of the ozone layer doubled skin cancer cases, 1981-91; caesium from the Chernobyl reactor polluted the hills in May 1986 and effluent from salmon-farming and oil polluted the seas....Had the time for the Scots to decide on their nationality simply come too late, when the dreams both of European union and of small nations were falling apart? But what was the alternative?

CHRISTOPHER HARVIE, *NO GODS AND PRECIOUS FEW HEROES* (1998)

Books cited or consulted include:

Bill Alexander, *British Volunteers for Liberty: Spain 1936-1939* (Lawrence and Wishart, 1982)

Valentine Cunningham, *The Penguin Book of Spanish Civil War Verse* (Penguin, 1980)

T M Devine, *The Scottish Nation 1700-2000* (Allen Lane, 1999)

Carol Ann Duffy, *Selling Manhattan* (Anvil Press, 1987)

Ronald Fraser, *Blood of Spain: The Experience of Civil War 1936-1939* (Allen Lane, 1979)

Nicholas Goodrick-Clarke, *Hitler's Priestess* (New York University Press, 1998)

Christopher Harvie, *No Gods and Precious Few Heroes: Twentieth-Century Scotland* (third edition, Edinburgh University Press, 1998)

Christopher Harvie, *Fool's Gold: The Story of North Sea Oil* (Hamish Hamilton, 1994)

John Hodge, *Trainspotting* (screenplay, Faber and Faber, 1996)

Kathleen Jamie, *The Queen of Sheba* (Bloodaxe Books, 1994)

Magnus Linklater and Robin Denniston, *Anatomy of Scotland* (Chambers, 1992)

Sorley MacLean, *From Wood to Ridge: Collected Poems in Gaelic and English* (Carcanet, 1989)

Andrew Marr, *The Battle for Scotland* (Penguin, 1992)

Naomi Mitchinson, *Oil for the Highlands?* (Fabian Society, 1974)

Edwin Muir, *Scottish Journey* (Mainstream, 1979)

RESEARCHED AND COMPILED BY DAVID JAYS

Victoria

for Annie

There really are times when the entire history of the world seems to me like one great shipwreck from which the only imperative is to rescue oneself.

Henrik Ibsen

> . . . I will go down to Hallaig
> to the sabbath of the dead,
> where the people are frequenting,
> every single generation gone.

Sorley Maclean

> Time present is a cataract whose force
> Breaks down the banks even at its source,
> And history forming in our hands.
> Not plasticene but roaring sands,
> Yet we must swing it to its final course.

John Cornford

Victoria was first performed by the Royal Shakespeare Company at the Pit, Barbican, on 17 April 2000. The company was as follows:

Tony Curran	Tom Watson
Scott Handy	Sarah Collier
Duncan Marwick	Morag Hood
Michael Nardone	Jackie Kane
Brian Pettifer	Anne Lacey
Derek Riddell	Neve McIntosh
Sean Scanlan	Hannah Miles

Directed by Ian Brown
Designed by Angela Davies
Lighting by Nigel Edwards
Music by Peter Salem
Movement by Caroline Salem
Assistant Director Ruth Levin
Company voicework by Lyn Darnley and Andrew Wade
Dialect Coach Charmian Hoare
Production Manager Simon Bourne
Stage Manager Michael Budmani
Deputy Stage Manager Maddy Grant
Assistant Stage Manager Jess Williams

Setting

The play is set in a rural place on the coast of Scotland. Part One is set in the autumn of 1936. Part Two is set in the spring of 1974. Part Three is set in the summer of 1996.

Doubling

The play is written to be performed by fourteen actors. No more than fourteen actors should be used. The character of Victoria must be played by the same actress throughout.

A note on punctuation

. . .
This tends to mean that the character has intended to complete the sentence but is either unwilling or unable to do so.

—
This tends to mean the character has jumped to a new thought, or suddenly jumped to silence.

dialogue continues on a new line
This asks the performer to take note of the rhythm of the speech. It can, but does not necessarily, imply a short beat.

Author's Note

I began work work on *Victoria* in 1996, during my period as Pearson writer in residence of the RSC. The work has since evolved through a number of drafts and it has developed and changed, much as I have, during that time. 1996 was a bleak, fag-ended year in Scotland, but it was also the year that my daughter was born and so, for me, a time of imagining the future as well as imagining the past.

Two images coalesced to spark the play's creation. The first was the image of a woman standing by a tree, smoking a cigarette and waiting for a man to arrive. The second came on a visit to an island off the west coast where I drank in the only pub. Also drinking that particular night, in that small room, were the owner of half the island and his guests, distillery workers from Glasgow, some hippie-ish refugees from city life and some old crofters who had lived and worked on the island all their lives. At the bar, I looked in the local telephone directory. There were eighty or so names in it.

The physical presence of history is unavoidable in towns and in cities. But perhaps in smaller places, places more remote from the capitals of nations, history is refracted and revealed in a different way, its effects inscribed more subtly on the landscape, and in sharper relief in the lives of the people. Of course, in the West Highlands, the twentieth century and its effects are set against a haunting absence brought about through clearance and emigration, and set also against the presence, in the mountains and sea, of a much larger geological time – both of which serve to contextualise the recent past and our dreams of the future.

Victoria began to be written when I realised that the young woman with the cigarette was standing in the woods in 1936, and that nearby, in 1996, was a pub in a place where the telephone directory occupied two sheets of A4.

I would like to like to thank the following people and organisations for their help, encouragement and advice during the writing of *Victoria*: Simon Reade, Ian Brown, Michael Boyd, Mel Kenyon, Colin Chambers, Dan Rebellato, David Harrower, Graham Eatough, Alan Wilkins, Suspect Culture and Lucie Macaulay.

Part One

THE BRIDE

Characters

Shona, *a kitchen maid.*
Victoria, *a minister's daughter.*
Oscar, *a prospective student.*
Callum, *a farmworker.*
Gavin, *a gamekeeper.*
Euan, *a farmworker.*
Margaret, *a middle-class English girl.*
David, *heir to the estate.*
Lord Allan, *owner of the estate.*
MacPhee, *a shipyard owner.*
Armitage, *a factory owner.*
Mrs MacPhee, *wife of a shipyard owner.*
Mrs Armitage, *wife of a factory owner.*
Mrs Wilson, *wife of a venture capitalist.*
Macallister, *a teacher.*

1

A tree.
Victoria *sitting on a stone.*
She takes out an old folded page of an illustrated magazine.
She pores over it.

Victoria   You and me.
One step across that water.
We'll be gone.
I'll carry you.
We're not waiting.
Wait any longer we'll be turned stone.

2

The Red House Lawn.
Mr *and* **Mrs Armitage**, **Mr** *and* **Mrs MacPhee**, **Miss
Wilson** *and* **Lord Allan**. *Standing beside a small cannon.*

MacPhee   Air. Sea. Great to be here, Hugh.
Looking forward to getting out on to the hill.
Cooped up in Glasgow.
The spirit dies. Dies.

Mrs Armitage   Gregor's looking forward to the stalking.
He's terribly eager to give it a go.

Armitage   Oh, can't wait.
Eager's the word for it all right.
Yes.

Mrs MacPhee   How have you found the girl, Margaret,
Lord Allan.

Mrs Armitage   English, isn't she?

Mrs Wilson   We don't know the family.
Do we know the family?

Lord Allan   They're from Kent, originally.

Mrs Wilson   Oh, Kent.
Kent.

Mrs Armitage   She'll be settling in, no doubt.
Getting to know the house.

Lord Allan   I'm afraid she's a little disappointed with the
house.

Mrs MacPhee   Well, she's bound to feel a little out of
place, Lord Allan.
The mountains, the sea, the forest.
The poor girl's used to London.

MacPhee   Terrible place.
Son went to the dogs there.
Had to drag him back before he ruined me.

Lord Allan   She commented on the furniture this
morning.

Mrs Armitage   She's young.
Every generation wants to shift things a little.
I know myself when we bought Tigh na Bruiach, I felt
compelled to have the curtains replaced.
It's a powerful urge but it fades with time.

Lord Allan   I'd never noticed before that we had
furniture, as such.
We simply . . . sat.

Armitage   Curtains.
More expensive than you think.

Mrs Wilson   She'll learn, Lord Allan, and what a place to
learn, so full of romance. This lovely gun, for example . . .

MacPhee   Good gun.
Must have been aimed at the – what – the French?
The Spanish?

Lord Allan   The Macleods.

Mrs Wilson   My nephew Gordon is a Macleod.

Mrs Armitage   I don't imagine for a moment that
Gordon would expect to be aimed at by a gun and so it is
with Margaret. Who could have known she was David's
target? Not you, not I, perhaps not even the boy himself.
One is bound to be surprised by the choices of one's
children, Lord Allan. But if the world contains these
surprising possibilities, what choice have the young but to
unearth them.

Lord Allan   Certainly I didn't send my son abroad in
order that he marry a woman, Mrs Armitage. A contessa, a
marquise, but not an ordinary woman.

MacPhee   Abroad.

Mrs Wilson   They met in Germany.

MacPhee   Terrible place.

Armitage   Very good porcelain.

Mrs MacPhee   The Allans have held the Red House for
three hundred years. I'm sure it will survive the enthusiasms
of the current season, however continental they may be.

3

The jetty.
Callum, **Gavin** *and* **Euan** *unloading boxes from the boat.*
Oscar *is investigating their contents.*

Oscar   Bedlinen. Silver. Sugar. Claret.

Gavin   Keep your hands off.

Oscar   Who's going to miss a bottle?

Callum   If he gets one. I get one.

Oscar   Fuck off.

Callum   Put it back then. It's not yours to take.

Euan   See and since you're here, Oscar, you might as well help.

Oscar   It's you that gets paid for it.

Gavin *is carrying a particularly heavy trunk.* **Oscar** *helps him. They put it down.*

Gavin   There's more boxes waiting over the bay. If you want work.
You can help shift them.

Oscar   I only want to see what they've brought back.
See what the world's got that we don't.

Callum   I'll come with you over the bay, Gav.

Gavin   Fair enough.

Oscar *opens the trunk.*

Euan   Leave it alone, Oscar.
You'll get us into bother.

Oscar   Knickers.
It's full of her underthings.
A box that size and it's only for a woman's delicates.

He shows the others.

Soft against your hand.
That's the way a woman's things ought to be.
Imagine an arse wrapped in that.
Silk on one side. Skin on the other.

Callum   Let's feel.

Oscar   Not for greedy boys.

Callum   Let's feel.

Oscar   This Callum, is the secret of a rich woman.
Smell.
This is the smell of a woman who doesn't sweat.
Whose sweat is perfume.
You'll not get that smell off a kitchen maid's scants.

This is a smell that belongs to the aristocracy alone.
This is privilege for you, Callum.
Very few working men have had this experience.
After the revolution, all women's clothes will smell of work.
That's why I'm not a socialist,
Because after the revolution, Callum,
All women will smell like your sister.

Euan   Put them back.

Callum   They're lovely.

Oscar   Better put them away before Callum faints.

Callum   No . . . it's just . . . silk like.
Must feel nice for the lassie.
That's all.

Oscar *puts the pants in his pocket and shuts the trunk carefully.*

Gavin   Are you coming over the bay or not?

Oscar   Sorry, Gav, I can't.

Gavin   C'mon, Cal, we'll go now and be back before it's
dark.
Leave that.

Callum   It's a shame right enough.

Gavin   He's just slagging you, Callum, don't worry about it.

Callum *and* **Gavin** leave.

Euan   See, Oscar, we're friends, but I want you to know.
I'd easy kill you.
If that was the order.
If that's what needed doing.

Oscar   You think I need shot?

Euan   You just talk.

Oscar   Christ, you're as bad as the minister.
Shoot me.
I wouldn't shoot you.

Euan   No discipline.
You just talk.

Oscar *puts a bottle of claret in his pocket.*
Oscar *leaves.*

4

In the Red House.
A large wireless.
Margaret *is sitting in a comfortable, modern armchair.*
She gets up and switches the wireless on.
The wireless receives only hiss.
She sits.
She pauses.
She rings a bell.
She gets up and tries to retune it.
A brief sparkle of classical music.
She sits.
Hiss.
She gets up.
Shona *enters.*
Margaret *switches off the wireless.*

Margaret   Hello.
Which one are you?

Shona   I'm Shona, madam.

Margaret   Shona.
That's right, isn't it.
I'm sure I'll remember everyone's name eventually.

Shona   I came to tell you, madam.
The boat's unloaded.

Margaret   Good. Thank you.
This thing, Shona, I wonder if you know anything about
reception?

Shona   No, madam.

Margaret   Do you have a wireless?

Shona   No, madam, some houses. Weven't got one.

Margaret   Maybe I can get one of the men to rig up some sort of aerial contraption.

Shona   Gavin'll do that for you, madam, if you want.

Margaret   Terrific. Gavin.
. . .
What do you think of the chair?
I bought it in London. I know it was extravagant to bring it all this way but I'm terribly in love with it and the furniture here's all so ancient. Do you want to try it out?
. . .
Try it out.

Shona *sits in it.*

Margaret   It's ultra modern.

Shona   Feels comfy right enough, madam.

Margaret   You know. Shona. If you don't mind, I might ask you to call me Margaret from now on. Because madam reminds me of my mother. I'd like us to be friends.
Wouldn't you?

Shona   Yes, madam.

Margaret   Margaret.
Or even . . . Marge.

Shona   Margaret.

Margaret   Do you have children, Shona?

Shona   No, m . . .

Margaret   Do you have a husband? A man you like?

Shona   . . .

Margaret   Oh, don't be embarrassed. I'm nosy. I just like to know everyone, that's all. I'm sure we'll get on famously.

Shona *gets out of the chair.*

Shona   There's a man I see.

Margaret   Who? Who? Do tell.

Shona   Gavin.

Margaret   Gavin. The wireless man. How lucky. He's
one of ours. When I was little we had a girl and she met a
man from a different house. They had to marry for love. It
was all such a wrench for everybody. We never saw her
again. It's lovely he's near you.

Shona   Is there anything else?

Margaret   No.
Just the wireless.
I'm sure David will make an appearance when he feels up to
it.
. . .
You know, I wondered about being lonely in this house.
But I don't think that can be possible.

Shona   You're a lucky woman, Margaret.
Your husband, I mean.
. . .
Saw him standing up in the boat on the way over.
Like a Viking coming here or something.
Lucky woman.
. . .
Sorry.

Margaret   No.
Don't apologise. It's a kind thing to say. I am lucky, really.
Aren't I? I really think so. I really do.

Shona *leaves.*
Margaret *switches the wireless on.*
A brief signal.
Hiss.
She sits.

5

The edge of the forest.
Victoria *waiting.*
Oscar *arrives.*

Oscar   Victoria.
You there?

Victoria   It's near dark. You said sooner.

Oscar   Look at you standing.

Victoria   I've been waiting.

Oscar   It's the same every time.
Each sight of you and I want you all over again.
Each time.
It's worth a song about it.

Victoria   Don't look at me like that.
I'm not yours to look at.
Don't eye me up.

Oscar   Something about your hair and the night being dark.
Maybe's the hill.
I've a tune.
But I've no words.

Victoria   Where were you?

Oscar   I was getting you a present.

He takes out a bottle of claret.

I've no glasses, so we'll need to take it from the bottle.

Victoria   You steal this?

Oscar   For you.

Victoria   You'll not be caught?

Oscar   Not me.

She takes the bottle and drinks some.

How come you called for me, Vic?
How come in the woods?
How come the evening?
S'it you can't resist me.

Victoria   My sister wrote me.

Oscar   What to say?

Victoria   Keep your hands off me.
Says there's a boat in Glasgow.

Oscar   Your skin.
What sister?

Victoria   Glasgow sister.
Oscar, listen.

Oscar   I'm listening.

Victoria   Says there's a boat at Greenock waiting to leave
for Argentina.
What're you doing?

Oscar   I have to. I have to do this.

Victoria   You're tearing them.

Oscar   I have to.
Once in my life.
Take my chance.

Oscar *tears her knickers.*

Victoria   What've you done?

Oscar   Our secret.

Victoria   There's no time.
I've to be at the manse soon, else they'll miss me.
If you'ld come when you said.

She pushes him away.

Oscar   Away, you go home then.
If you want.

Victoria   My sister says the boat's taking folk on.
To work.

Oscar   Which boat?

Victoria   The Argentina boat. The liner.

He tries again.

What's in you tonight. You're worse even than usual.

Oscar   I brought these for you.

He takes the knickers out of his pocket. Gives them to her.

Victoria   Who's these?

Oscar   Yours.
Stole them too.

Victoria   These're beautiful, Oscar.
Silk.
Silk and claret.
You little thief.

Oscar   Put them on.

She puts the knickers on.
He watches.

Victoria   The liner's hiring, and she says they've an
orchestra to make and a need for chambermaids. My sister's
doing the roster. So she's says we've only to get to Glasgow
and we've got work.

Oscar   What you wanting ship work for?

Victoria   I'm wanting away from here, Oscar, wanting
over the water. Like we said.

Oscar   When d'we say?

Victoria   Here, night of the drinking.

Oscar   Oh aye. So we did.

Victoria   Argentina's soil so deep you can dig for a day
and never hit a stone. Cities better than Paris, and cinemas
and newness. She sent me the picture. What's here, Oscar?
A scraping of land on top of rock, and . . . a weight of
oldness. They told us folk wept to leave it but who'd you see
coming back. World's moving. People moving, we've only
to cross the sea. Same sea we're looking at. The world's
waiting for us, we've only to take our places in it. You and
me. Just to see ourselves in a place that isn't here. The
thought of it's like breathing again. Like waking up.
Will you come ?

Oscar   There's a summer of work left.

She goes to him. Kisses him.

Victoria   There's nobody else like us here.
Nobody half as quick.
Can't be accident, can it?
Two of us.
Same village.
Must be meant. Must be . . .

Oscar   Pure luck. Your luck. My luck.

Victoria   You and talking.
You just talk.
You could smoke away your life with that talk and still be
sat here when you're old.
Still the same.

Oscar   You told your father this?
Told your mother?

Victoria   Course not.
They'd have me kept.
Have me married to a theological student and mansed all
my life, like my mother.

Oscar   You half look like her.
See, with your mouth – your eyes.

Dressed in black at the back of the kirk.
Black rock she is.

Victoria   Twenty years of kirk and winter and she's had.
Time's took her looks from her.
I'll not be my mother.

She stands up.

I'm late. They'll be wondering where I am.
I'm catching that boat, Oscar.
Will you come with me?

Oscar   Aye, I'll come.
I'll try Argentina.
See what's there for me.

Oscar *takes out his fiddle.*
Starts to play a tune.

Victoria   S'pretty.
What is it?

Oscar   It's my new tune, coming to me just now.
Smell you on my fingers as I'm playing.
I call it,
'Lament for Victoria's Cunt'
It's a tribute.
I'll play it tomorrow night at the ceilidh for the boy's
wedding.
Obviously I won't announce its full title.
That's between you and me.

6

The jetty, late evening.
Callum, **Euan** *and* **Gavin**.
In the distance, **David** *with a bottle.*

Gavin   Smoke?

Euan   No.

Gavin   Aye.

Euan   What's he doing?

Callum   Looking at the loch.

Gavin   The stalking party tomorrow, Euan, they're city people, not great shots. I've left the hinds' hay up in the corrie so they'll be hanging around waiting to be shot at. You'ld be as well taking a gun up yourself, you can wait on the ridge and if there's any they hit badly, you can finish them off.

Callum   He doesn't look very happy, considering it's him that's newly wed.

Euan   I took him over this morning.
Carried his books for him.
See how she had trunks and cases.
He'd only books. I took them under my arm to keep the water off. Like I was a schoolboy.
See the books he had.
I noticed.
Mostly German.

Callum   German books.
German submarines it'll be next.

Gavin   What?

Callum   German submarines it'll be. Coming up the loch.

Gavin   How? Where'll they be going?

Callum   Divers.
He'll have made contact with them.
A signal.
Using the moon and mirrors.
And they'll be coming.

Gavin   German divers coming here?
What for, the stalking?

Callum   To invade, Gav. What else is he waiting for with his bottle and his books?

Euan   He's looking at the water like he's a mind to walk into it.

Gavin   Germans'll not invade here, Cal.

Callum   How not?

Gavin   There's nothing here they'd want.

Callum   We've got women.

Gavin   The Germans have got women of their own.

Callum   You'ld not say that if they came for your sister.

Gavin   I've not got a sister.

Callum   I have.

Gavin   Big Helen.

Euan   He's looking at us.

Gavin   Norman over at Dubh Loch's more of a danger to Big Helen than any German.

Callum   That's not what Macallister says.

Gavin   What does Macallister say?

Euan   Now he's looking back at the sea.

Callum   Macallister says the fascists are on the march.
They're moving.
We should be getting ready to fight them.

Gavin   I'm not a German, Callum.
But I'd not come between Norman and Big Helen.
Not for any cause.

Callum   He's waiting for a signal. A signal's coming and I'm going to be ready for it. S'all I'm telling you.

Euan   He's coming over.

Gavin   What's he want?
I'm having a smoke, fuck's sake.

Callum   Fuck's sake.

They look at him. He stops. He dawdles.

Gavin   I can't smoke with that fucker watching me.

Euan   Loch's that still tonight.
Him with a bottle.
I'd do that.
If it was mine.
I'd look at the water sometimes.

Callum   He's coming over.

David *approaches. Sits with them.*

David   Lads.
Drink . . . ?

Gavin   No thank you, sir.

Euan   I'll take one.

Callum   Thanks.

They drink from the bottle.

David   Mild still. The water's . . . glassy.
One can see oneself reflected.
You know – I've been thinking –
I saw you there and I was thinking.
This moonlight, glass water, still mild night.
Would do for my stag night.
. . .
Never did have a stag night.
And so I need some chaps to drink with.

He drinks.

To freedom.
To a last night of freedom on this earth.

Euan   Congratulations.

Gavin   Aye, congratulations, sir.

Callum   Congratulations.

David   You know, it's four years since I last stood here
and watched the loch.
I love the sound of it.
. . .
Look at you looking at me.
. . .
Tell me a dirty story.
It's my stag night.

Callum   I don't know any, sir.

David   Yes you do.
You fucking do.
Sorry.
I'm sorry.
I'll start. I'll tell a story.
. . .
This is the story of how I put my little manservant up a
whore's arse. I was in Berlin. Something I had always
wanted to do.
Can you believe it, in Berlin brothels they have it on the
menu. They call it – Greek.
. . .
Some of the officer boys I was with took me.
What do you think of that?
Quite a story.
. . .
You're uncomfortable with me.
Please don't be.
Please feel free to be easy with me.
. . .
Four years I've been across Europe. Nothing's changed here.
Same sounds. Same water lapping. You'ld be amazed if
you'ld seen what I'd seen. Truly amazed. Waves in Berlin.
Water lapping here.
. . .
Have more drink.

Gavin   Thank you, sir.

They all drink.

David   Can I tell you a secret?
. . .
I look at myself reflected in this water and I despair.
. . .
You lads have such perfect poker faces.
What's going on in your heads?
Quiet and thinking.
Or are they empty?
. . .
But Gavin.
How's Shona?
Are you two the handsomest couple in the country?
My wife tells me she's sweet on you.
Is she well?

Gavin   She's well, sir. Thank you.

David   She's a very beautiful woman.
Physically.
Very fit.
Because she works. She works, you see.
She's uncorrupted by the ease which has eroded me.
Do you know what the tragedy is?
Three hundred years ago you would have admired me.
Three hundred years ago I would have been admirable.
You a clan and me your captain.
Look at us now.
This rotting jetty.
If we all slipped into the sea what difference would it
make.
I am the last damaged specimen of a once admirable seed.
You lads – looking at me.
I've no plans to continue the line you'll be pleased to know.
I'll fertilise only bowels.
I'm not queer.
Just . . .

Patriotic.
Let's put the boat out, shall we, let's go out on the water.

Callum   . . .

Gavin   Sir . . . I think.

Callum   It's late, sir.

Gavin   It wouldn't be wise with the drink.

David   What?
It'll be a lark.
Come on, chaps.

Euan   I'll put the boat out, Gav.
You and Cal go home.
I'll do it.

David   Put the boat out.
It's my stag night and it's mild still.
The loch is . . .
And I do own it.

Gavin   Night, sir.

Callum   Night.

Euan *starts to drag the rowing boat out of the boathouse.*

David   Look at this.
Mountains, sea and forest.
To be employed by a man like me.
Must fill you with despair.

Euan   You should sit, sir.
You're seeming unsteady.

David   Do you have any illnesses, Euan?

Euan   No, sir.
Sit down, sir.

The boat is out. **Euan** *tries to get* **David** *to sit in it.*
David *steps into it but remains standing.*
He wobbles.

Falls.
Euan *helps him up.*
He gets back in the boat.
He sits.

David   I've been to Germany, Euan.

Euan   So I heard, sir.

David   There's strength in Germany.

Euan   So they say.

David   I met men in Germany who educated me.
They told me about things, things which amazed me.
Things we don't know about yet.
About the Dravids and the Aryans, and the fires of the
goddess Kali and the purity that she brings from ashes.
Wisdom, Euan, beauty. I had this done in Mecklenburg. It's
a Hindu symbol.

Shows **Euan** *a swastika tattooed on his forearm.*

And we have the arrogance to think we rule India. A
thousand years of unbroken civilisation. The Brahmins, the
Kshatriyas, the Sudras, and the sacred Aryan lands. We
dare to trample that ground with vulgar Christianity. Do
you believe in God, Euan?

Euan   No, sir.

David   Good.
The Christ God, the Jew God.
Who – what? Promises to save?
When all around us is the power of nature and time.
The universe would waste a thought on us?
Are you a nationalist, Euan?

Euan   No, sir.

David   Are you a socialist?

Euan   I don't know, sir.

David   Yes you fucking do.

You know.
You are one.
Let me tell you a secret.
I am a nationalist.
I am a socialist.
I am a national socialist.
I believe in the nation. In the aristocracy of working men.
Mountains, sea and forest.
A working man like you, Euan, is the purest stock.
Men like me are degraded. Biological waste.
Do you drink?

Euan   Not much, sir.

David   Good, good. Do you like women?

Euan   In what way, sir?

David   In a sexual way.

Euan   I like women enough.

David   Good.
Take the boat out.

Euan   Maybe we should leave it, sir.
The weather can change.

David   The forces are gathering, Euan. This is what I
learned in Germany. An avatar has come.
The clouds are coming off the Atlantic to meet the hill.
The forces of the north, the pure, against the forces of the
degenerate, the civilised, the carriers of disease.
There will be a fire.
A magnificent fire.
Corpses will be interred and their blood will enrich the soil.
Your corpse may be one of them.
Mine certainly will.
I want it.
Take me out now.
Take me out on to the loch.

Euan *pushes out the boat.*

7

Bright morning.
High on the mountainside.
Lord Allan, **Armitage** *and* **MacPhee** *stalking.*
Gavin *is with them.*
They speak in whispers, move slowly.

Armitage   Boy decide not to come then, Hugh?

Lord Allan   He has a hangover. He remained in bed.

MacPhee   Wind. Fresh air's the best cure for over-
indulgence.
Rips your guts open and scours you clean.

Lord Allan   He's been left to sleep it off.

MacPhee   You should have made him walk it off.

Armitage   Poor lad. He's got all his married life ahead of
him.
Let him sleep.

Lord Allan   We haven't spoken except to exchange words
on his condition this morning. He has done his best to keep
himself away from my society since his return.
He's cowering.

MacPhee   As well he might.

Armitage   Wish I was in bed.
It's bloody cold.

Gavin   Gentlemen. Over here.
There.
See.

They approach **Gavin**.

MacPhee   Hinds are they?

Gavin   Hinds and calves.
Stags there. Watching.

MacPhee   There he is, I can see the bugger.

Gavin   In the lee, above the burn, top end of the corrie.

Armitage   Tipple anyone?

Offers a silver flask of whisky. No one takes. He does.

Engraved.
Got it in Glasgow.
Got all the kit.
Tweeds . . .

Gavin   Quiet.

Armitage   Sorry.

Gavin   We'd best get down now. Go forward low.

They crouch. Some prone and edge forwards on their elbows.

Armitage   Up a hill. Following boots. Up we go.

MacPhee   Great stuff, Gavin. Great stuff.

Armitage   Your thoughts get into a rhythm, don't they?
Very philosophical business.
What a view. What a view.

MacPhee   We could do with a man like Gavin at our
place.
You wouldn't consider an offer, would you?

Lord Allan   Gavin inherited the position, Tom. It's in the
family.
The mountain's in his blood.

MacPhee   I can offer a fair sum.

Armitage   I can imagine, if I had an estate, I'm
considering buying, you know, crawling up a hill purely to
think. Clear the head.
Is anyone chilly?

Gavin   We're downwind, he's not seen us.

Armitage   I am, just a bit –

Gavin   We'll get in a bit closer.

MacPhee   Steady there, I've got him in my sights.

Armitage   Sorry.
Oh, I see him.
There he is.
Chewing his cud.
Digesting his breakfast.
Seems a peaceable sort of chap.
Poor fellow.

Lord Allan   What are we taking today, Gavin?

Gavin   One stag. Four hinds.

Lord Allan   You spotted the stag first, Tom. You want him?

MacPhee   Very much, Hugh.
I want that big bugger very much indeed.

Lord Allan   The rest of us can take hinds.

They all load cartridges into their guns, except **Armitage**.

Armitage   Bracing.
That's what it is.
Any ideas on estates, Tom? – the wife's keen.

Euan *enters with* **Victoria**, *another part of the hill.* **Euan**
carrying a gun.

Euan   Here.
You need to be working soon?

Victoria   Not for a while.

Euan   I wanted to talk to you. Alone.

He crouches right down. Gestures for her to do the same.

There they are.

Victoria   Look at you.
Belly in the heather.
Perfect.

You belong here.
There's lassies that've wrote songs for less than you.

Euan   You'll need to sit in case they see us.

She sits.

I wanted to talk to you, Victoria, because I've had an idea
about your situation.

Victoria   My job?

Euan   About your condition.

Victoria   What condition?

Euan   You've a baby coming.
I know.

Victoria   How?

Euan   I've seen you.
Sickening.
Trying to keep it hid.
I've watched you.
Way you've been lately.
Am I right?

Victoria   You been stalking me like a hind?

Euan   Am I right?

Victoria   What if you are?

Euan   It's not easy for me to speak about this, Victoria.

Victoria   Don't speak about it.
Speak about guns and deer.
Speak about things you know.

Euan   I know.
An accident of drinking.
Walking in the woods with someone.
Doesn't matter who.
Too much drink between you – and now – you're stuck.
You're not the first it's happened to.

Victoria   Said best leave it, Euan.

Euan   You can't leave it, Victoria.
Your father's the minister.
You can't leave a child growing in you and not speak
of it.
But the thing is – I've had an idea –
Victoria –
Because I've always had a – feeling for you, Victoria.

Victoria   I know.

Euan   Had it long as I can remember.

Victoria   I know.

Euan   The whole of the thing is I'm in love with you.

Victoria   You needn't say.

Euan   I don't think you know how much I am.

Victoria   I do.
I promise I know.

Euan   So my idea was –
I'm a good man – good for you.
And the child you're carrying –
So I thought, because I know you don't care for me.

Victoria   Never said I didn't care for you.

Euan   I thought we could make an arrangement where I
marry you.
I marry you, Victoria, so the child's fathered.
And – and –
If it's secret, Victoria, you can see whoever you want.
I'm not trying to trap you.
You see what I'm offering you?
Because I believe, I really believe that this wildness in you
will pass. And when it does. There'll be me.
And I'll have waited.

Victoria   I can't, Euan.

Euan The village'll not have you.
Not with a bastard in you.

Victoria Maybe's I don't want the village.

Euan Be daft.
Everyone knows I'm soft for you.
I'm trying to help you.

Victoria Maybe's I'll go over the water.

Euan You've no money to go.

Victoria Talk about something else, Euan.
It's not right to waste your thinking on me.

Euan S'the father to look after you?
S'he to marry you?
S'he know?

Victoria S'it matter?

Euan You'll go with any man but you won't go with me.
S'that it?

Victoria Maybes.

Euan And I'm the one who loves you best.
What? Am I uglier? I don't think so.
Other lassies say not.

Victoria Any man but you.

Euan What is it?
What's it that's in your head?

Victoria You're the best of this place, Euan.
Always have been. Brother to me.
You'ld keep me.
You'ld soften the want I have to run.
Year and year I'd have your kindness over me like a
blanket.
Size of the mountains here.
Depth of the loch.
What am I to them?

Time there's been before me, and time there'll be after,
makes me nothing.
Turns me stone.
You'd keep me here, Euan.
I need to go somewhere's not seen the like of me.

Euan   Selfishness it is.
You're young but –
Other men you've seen, these ways of thinking they've give
you.
They'll go. They'll all go.
I'll wait till I'm old, Vic, when I'm sixty waiting, when I'm
eighty. If I've strength left in my body. You're in me – your
face – the mind of you – you cross the sea I'll wait till you
come back – you die and I'll wait like a dog on the grave,
Victoria, – I'll wait for you.

With the gentlemen on the hill.

Lord Allan   Are you ready, Gregor?
We're shooting now.

Armitage   Righto. Ready. Ready over here.

Gavin   When we shoot, any that're not hit will run down
towards the burn over there. As soon as you've fired, follow
them down with the sights.
Whenever you're ready, gentlemen.

Lord Allan   All set.

A barrage.
Euan *and* **Victoria** *hear the barrage.*

Euan   Shit.
Silly fucker's got its leg.
Poor beast.

Euan *shoots.*

MacPhee   A beauty.
An absolute god.
Clean kill.
. . .
Congratulations, me.

They all shake hands with **MacPhee**.
During the barrage, **Victoria** *has gone.*
Euan *hasn't noticed.*

Euan   Bastard's missed.
There's a hind wounded and she's gone amongst the trees.
Fuck.
Beast's trailing mess behind her.

8

Late morning.
The lawn of the Red House.

Margaret, **Mrs MacPhee**, **Mrs Wilson** *and* **Mrs Armitage** *having tea at an outdoor table.*

Mrs MacPhee   How are you finding Scotland, Margaret, we certainly are different here, aren't we?

Margaret   Oh, Scotland's wonderful, Mrs MacPhee, I only wish my mother and father could have had a chance to see it.

Mrs Armitage   Darling, we're not at the pole.
One doesn't have to be Shackleton.
Surely they can visit?

Margaret   They're dead.
They died in India.
Ferozpur.

Mrs Armitage   Oh, my dear, the way you speak.
So plainly.
Doesn't she speak plainly?

Mrs Wilson   Very.

Margaret   I pride myself on it, Lily, I speak as plainly as I can.

Mrs MacPhee   Ferozpur – I know a couple in Ferozpur.

Margaret   I was born there, perhaps I know them?

Mrs MacPhee   Oh, I doubt it. He used to be a doctor.
A lovely Jewish man who went by the name of Allbright
in Hyndland. He had such manageable hands. My new
doctor's from Edinburgh and he pushes and pulls at me
as though I were a side of beef. Do you have a doctor
yet? We'll need to arrange it for you – a Glasgow
man.

Margaret   I don't think I met an Allbright.

Mrs MacPhee   He became involved in some form of
politics and went a bit – funny, I'm afraid.

Mrs Armitage   Well, you'll have cast an eye over the
house already, Margaret. There'll be so much to do with an
old place like this. Have you been to Edinburgh for the
shops?

Margaret   As a matter of fact, I haven't, Lily.

Mrs Wilson   Oh, you must.
It's essential.

Margaret   I've been concentrating my mind on other
plans.

Mrs Armitage   Sounds wonderful, do tell.

Margaret   I intend to build a causeway over the lake.

Mrs Wilson   Over the loch?

Mrs MacPhee   A causeway? That's not very
decorative.

Margaret   I assure you I have no intentions of it being
decorative, Mrs MacPhee.

Mrs Armitage   I was wondering more whether you had
plans for the dining room.

Margaret   You ladies came here by steamer from
Glasgow?

Mrs Armitage   It was a glorious trip, Margaret.

Mrs Macphee   It's my husband's steamer.
He's a keen sailor.

Mrs Armitage   The islands, really – weren't they, Claire
– we could have been cruising in the Peloponnese.

Margaret   Well, it takes for ever to get here overland.
The train only takes you as far as Achnasheen and then the
car has to come over the hills, and finally, everything has to
be unloaded again and carried over on the boats.
Which slows us down.
The people here are backward. They've been left behind.
They haven't the chances of city people.

Mrs Wilson   Have you asked them whether they want a
causeway?

Margaret   I'm sure they do.

Mrs MacPhee   At least they have their health.
Glasgow people are so wan and stunted. They barely see
the sunlight. When they lift a slice of bread it's black with
fingerprints.
It can't be healthy.

Margaret   A causeway will speed things up.
That way these people won't have to move to Glasgow.
I saw it as soon as I arrived.

Mrs Armitage   It sounds positively intriguing. Perhaps
David could ask Mr Wilson to build it for you. His firm
specialises in these areas. Doesn't it?

Margaret   I'll certainly talk to him about it.

Mrs MacPhee   Now where is David, Margaret?
He surely hasn't abandoned you already?

Margaret   I believe he went up to the hill –
Walking – He's in training for our honeymoon.

Mrs Wilson   Walking?

Margaret   We're going to Bavaria. David's friendly with
a duke and we've been invited to spend the summer in the
high mountains. David's passionate about mountains.
The higher the better as far as he's concerned.

Mrs Wilson   Mountains. Causeways.
I thought the modern generation were supposed to have
fallen into decadence.
But it seems to me they're becoming positively Scandinavian.

9

Inside a wooden shed, windows shut.
Small amounts of light.
Amongst guns and hung grouse.
Euan *teaching* **Oscar** *how to clean a gun.*
Oscar *watching.*

Euan   A fire – s'what he said – blood and corpses.
He was drinking – else he'd not have told me.

Oscar   He's lost it. King of some mad place. Some place
abroad.

Euan   Concentrate –
It's important it's clean.

Oscar   He's maybes insane – syphilitic.

Euan   Boy's not mad – it's how it is now for his class.

Oscar   Probably caught it from travelling Germany.

Euan   It was his grandfather cleared this estate.
Half Canada's there because of the Allans.

Oscar   Consorting with students and whores on the banks
of the Rhine.

Euan   It's Allan schoolmasters that belt you for not
speaking English.

Oscar   I wouldn't mind catching a bit syphilis.

Euan   Allan ministers they put in the kirk.

Oscar   At least to get the chance to catch it.

Euan   He's the owner of the land.
He's to keep it for himself and his children.
That's the side he's on.
Side we're on's different.
Fire's war. That's all.
He's saying there's a war to come.
And I'm to fight in it.
He's not mad.

Oscar   War?
You been talking to Macallister?

Euan   I know my own mind.

Oscar   You're a village boy, Euan.
I'm the one's always been looking to go away.

Euan   Aye, well.
Maybe's there's not much for me here any more.

Oscar   Victoria's here.
You said to me you were going to get her to marry you.

Euan   She said no.

Oscar   You asked her?

Euan   Today.
Lassie doesn't know her own mind.

Oscar   You're made for her.
Try again.
You've no need to go throwing yourself into combat over it.

Euan   Oscar, you're my friend.

Oscar   Aye.

Euan   I can tell you this.
She's another man's child in her.
She'll not have me.

Oscar   She told you this.

Euan   Aye, on the hill.

Oscar   She said the father's name?

Euan   No.
Some man doesn't care for her.
Some thief.
She's talking about going across the water.
Daftness.
She decided me.
Nothing to stay for.
I'm going.

Oscar   How're you getting to Spain?

Euan   We've to make our way to Edinburgh. There's a
Communist Party office there, and we'll be given passports
and all the documents we need. Then at Leith there's a boat
taking coal to Biarritz. We'll be given work on the boat, the
captain's a Basque so he's a sympathiser. Macallister says a
few of the Scots boys have gone across that way already.
This is what he told me. Then we'll join some others who'll
be waiting and they'll take us over the mountains into
Spain. Hold that.

Gives **Oscar** *a gun.*

Do you know how to hold it properly?

Oscar   Aye.

Euan   No you don't.
You don't grip it. You don't try to choke it.
You let it lie in your arms.
It has its own weight.
There.

Oscar   How do you get across the mountains?
Pyrenees are big enough mountains are they not?
Bigger than ours.

Euan   Mountain's a mountain.

There's guides who take us over, they know the sheep trails and the bothies – they'll take us in till we get to the Spanish side. Then we'll be met, we'll be signed up to the British Battallion and we'll be told what to do next. Macallister reckons we'll be sent to San Sebastian.

Oscar   In the paper they said the British have dug lines around Huesca.

Euan   When did you see a paper?

Oscar   It was a line or two in the *Scotsman*.
Jeanie's sister had used a page to wrap her hat when she came back from Perth for Ally's funeral.

Euan   Let the weight of it sit.
And then you use the sight to . . .
Can you see?

Oscar   I need my glasses on.

Euan   Where's Huesca?

Oscar   It wasn't marked in the school atlas.
I thought you'd know.

Euan   I know why I'm going.
I don't know where I'm going.

Oscar   You joining the party?

Euan   Macallister's asked me.
Might do.
All I know's there's a fight coming.
And I'm sick of those bastards winning.

Oscar   Bastards with claret and silky drawers.

Euan   Aye.

Oscar   So.
When do we go?

Euan   You want to come?

Oscar   Come for the crack.

Aye.
Why not?

Euan   You're all talk.

Oscar   I've said I'm coming.
I'm coming with you.

Euan   Day after tomorrow. Early.
You need to look more closely.
It takes patience, Osc.
Because if there's dirt. Even the smallest amount.
It'll explode in your face.
Or not work.
Which could have the same effect.
In the matter of keeping yourself alive.

Oscar   The cross is in the middle.

Euan   The cross should be just above what you want to hit.
Put your glasses on.
There. You've got it.
Pull the trigger.

Oscar   Oh . . . oh . . .

Euan   It's not going to bite you.

Oscar *pulls the trigger. Click.*

10

Amongst the forest.
Shona *searching.*

Shona   Here, dog!
Here, dog!
Come, dog!
Come, dog!

*Sees **David** sitting on a stone.*
He's naked.

Oh. Oh, sir.

Shona *turns to leave.*

David   Don't go, Shona, stay.
I didn't mean to frighten you.
This is just my natural state.
Nothing to be afraid of.

Shona   Victoria says you said the dog was lost.
Says you wanted me to call for it in the wood.

David   Look at me, Shona, don't talk to me looking away.

Shona   Sorry, sir, thought you'ld be stalking, sir.

David   Don't call me sir. I've known you since I was a child.
Call me David.

Shona   Sorry, sir. David.
Oh, well. Dog's mebbe lost.
I should get back.

David   You're laughing.

Shona   Can't help it.

David   It's ugly.

Shona   Sorry.

David   Clothes, Shona, make me the master – don't leave – and you the servant. I've taken off my clothes. I want you to do the same. Then we'll be simply a man and a woman here.

Shona   Sir?

David   David.

Shona   I can't take my clothes off.

David   I believe in nature, Shona, not in artifice.
Do it.

Shona   No, sir. I can't I just . . . Your wife.

David   I want you.
Not my wife.
My wife is nothing compared to you.
She has no flesh or blood.
She's drained. My desire for you is natural.
Healthy.
The desire of a man to possess. Your desire to be possessed.

Shona *is frozen. She remains for some time with her back to him.*

David   Start with your shoes.

She takes off her shoes.

Feel your skin against the stone.
That's how you're made to be.
Now your dress.

She takes her dress off.

Doesn't that feel better. Don't you feel stronger now.
Sit beside me.
Now look at us.
We're gods. I'm Loki and you're Hildegard.
Your people are descended from the Norse.
Your hair, your features, those are Norse features.
Those gods still live in you.
You're carved from ice.
Look down there.
How do you feel?

Shona   I know it's mad, like, sir. But it's nice as well. My bum on the grass.

David   It is nice, isn't it? This is called naturism. The practice of loving nature.

Shona   I need to get dressed. Shouldn't have done this. This is wrong.

David   That's why we have to do it.

Shona   I wish I was a different lassie, sir. And not known
you since you were little. And I wish it was a different time,
sir. But I can't. I'm with Gavin and . . .

David   You want me.

Shona   . . .

David   Answer me.

Shona *gets up, unsure, and starts to put her clothes on again.*

Shona   No.
I don't.

David   Stand still.
Don't be ashamed.
Nature's not ashamed of you.
Feel the air cover you up.
Let your arms drop.

Shona *drops her arms.*
Turns towards him.
David *takes a camera, ready, from a bag beside him.*

Shona   's that a camera?

He takes a photograph.

David   It's called a Box Brownie, Shona.
I took it with me all over Europe to record the power of
nature. I've taken your picture with it as a keepsake.
Now come and sit with me in the sunshine.

11

At the table.

Margaret   A causeway, Lord Allan,
I was telling the ladies how I intend to build a causeway
across the lake. I was telling them about my plans to
modernise the estate and the village. As soon as we come
back from Bavaria. I believe it will make quite a difference.
. . .

Of course, David will go into the mountains at the earliest
opportunity. I'm sure he finds weddings, even his own, very
dull. I believe one day we will live in a society where people
will never get married at all, they'll simply register their
names with a civil servant.

. . .

I believe one day we will live in a society where simply
everything is registered with civil servants. Where we don't
even have to look after ourselves at all because civil servants
will do everything. I believe we will live in a society one day
where nobody will have domestic help. Because servants will
have been entirely replaced by civil servants.

. . .

David was telling me these things when we met in Bayreuth.
He told me he was a modernist. And I said to him, If being
modernist means wanting things to become more modern
then I'm a modernist too.

. . .

Still . . . I think he cherishes the solitude one finds in remoter
places. Social occasions seem like a burden to him. And to
me. To me as well. I find socialising so trivial sometimes,
don't you, so, frustrating – like a fog. An awful fog.

12

The Red House kitchen.
Victoria *is cutting up venison.*
Shona *enters.*

In an adjacent room, **Gavin** *is trying to tune the wireless. Snatches of
white noise, music, voices can be heard as he works.*
During the scene he will hear **Shona**'s *voice.*
He will listen.

Victoria   Where've you been? I've had to do this myself.
Served at the table myself.
Boy never turned up.
Lassie was mortified.

Shona *moves, helps her.*

Shona   Imagine not eating at your own table.
The boy's lost.
Something abroad's taken him.

Victoria   The woman didn't know what to say.
Took it dignified, like.
Starched her face like she was born to it.
You going to the ceilidh?
You'll need to be getting ready.

Shona   What did folk eat?

Victoria   Ate everything.

Shona   Did they eat my soup? Did they like it?

Victoria   They liked it fine.

Shona   Poor woman.

Victoria   Silly bitch for coming here.

She realises that **Shona** *is upset.*

What's happened?

Shona   . . .
He lied.

Victoria   Who?

Shona   Dog was never lost.
He was waiting for me.

Victoria   The boy?
No.

Shona   Waiting for me in the wood.
. . .
I walked down the hill after.
Couldn't even run.
Didn't even want to run.
I was just wanting to fall in the bog and be drowned.
I'm angry, Vicky.

Victoria   He made you?
You seen Gavin?

Shona   No.
Seen nobody.

Victoria *holds* **Shona**.

Victoria   This place.
This place.

Shona   Tell nobody.
I'll lose my job, I'll need to leave.
I don't want to leave.
You tell nobody.
Understand?

Victoria   I'll not tell.

Shona   I'm angry.
I'm angry enough to kill him.

Victoria *holds* **Shona**.

Victoria   Nothing happened.
You dreamed it.
A thing's done in this place, it's as well to be a dream to you.
He's gone tomorrow.
He's gone tomorrow.
You'll still be here.

White noise.

13

The ceilidh.
Oscar *playing 'Lament for Victoria's Cunt' on the fiddle.*
Dancing. Drinking.
Gavin *standing alone with a bottle.*
Callum *is talking to* **Macallister**.
He takes out a revolver.

Callum   Mr Macallister.
I've been thinking about what you've been saying.
About being prepared.
About needing to be ready to strike.
And I wanted you to know.
I am.

Callum *pulls out a revolver.*

Macallister   For God's sake, boy, put that thing away.

Callum   It's a gun, Mr Macallister.
For the cause.

Macallister   Is it loaded?

Callum   No, sir, but I've got the right bullets.

Macallister   What are you showing it me for, boy?

Callum   I wanted you to know.
I'm prepared. When the signal comes.
When we move.
You can rely on me.
I took it from the house during the party.
Nobody saw me if that's what you're thinking.
They were too busy eating.

Macallister   All right, boy, good work. Well done.
Give the gun to me.

Callum   But, Mr Macallister. It's my weapon.

Macallister   Needs greater for it elsewhere.
Give it here.
I'll send it to Spain straight away.
This gun'll kill General Franco himself.
Don't you worry.
Now.
We're attracting attention to ourselves.
Best you go back to the dancing.
Nobody should know about our plans.

Callum   Secrecy, comrade.

Macallister   Right, son.

Callum   I understand.

Victoria *and* **Shona** *enter.*
Shona *sees* **Gavin***.*
A moment together.
She kisses him.

Shona   Did you eat?

Gavin   Aye.

Shona   Was the food good, like?
I'd no appetite.
You know what folk say.
If you cook it you never want it.

Gavin   It was good, aye.

Shona   Had the soup kept its taste?
Even the whole day?

Gavin   Kept its taste well.

Shona   That's a good thing.

Gavin   You'll be tired.

Shona   I'm not tired.

Gavin   We've no need to stay at the dance.

Shona   I've only just come.
I want to stay.

Gavin   We'll stay then.

Victoria *approaches* **Oscar***. He stops playing.*

Victoria   C'mon outside with me.

She takes his hand and puts it into her dress.

Oscar   Not here.

Victoria   Quick, do it.

She embraces him, kissing him quickly, directing his hand to the right place.

Oscar   Silk?

Victoria   For a wedding night.

Oscar   You wear silk for the laird's wedding?

Victoria   Our wedding.
C'mon, we'll get drunk.

Shona *and* **Gavin**.

Shona   Say something to me.
You're quiet, Gav.
Don't be quiet.

Gavin   I don't know what to say.

Shona   Tell me what you'll do tomorrow.
Tell me that.

Gavin   Tomorrow?
I've to go up the mountain, there's a hind injured and she needs taken down.

Shona   What happened to her?

Gavin   Wounded in the shoot. Couldn't finish her.

Shona   Will she heal?

Gavin   That's what I'll see.

Shona   Then what?

Gavin   Then I'll go to the boats.
There's an engine needing fixed.

Shona   What's it take to fix it?

Gavin   This is daft.

Shona   Tell.

Gavin   You take it apart. See which parts need mending.
Clean it.

Once it's cleaned you put it back together. Test it.

Shona   What'll you do then, Gav, after that?

Gavin   After that I'll come up to the house and find you.

Oscar *and* **Victoria**. *She makes to kiss him. He stops her.*

Oscar   What's in you?

Victoria   I want to.

Oscar   Someone'll see us.

Victoria   They're drinking.
If anyone sees we'll be gone tomorrow.

Oscar   Tomorrow?

Victoria   Tomorrow morning.
Not staying here a minute more.
I'll not be caught.
C'mon, we'll go to the woods.

Oscar   Now.

Victoria   Now.

David *passes them. Enters the ceilidh hall wearing a kilt and formal dress. The room falls silent.* **Shona** *wants to leave but* **David** *is blocking her exit. She moves into the crowd.*

David   Please . . . don't stop the party on my account.
I . . .
Public speaking has never been my . . .
I ought to say, on behalf of my wife and myself . . .
Thank you.
For your work in making our homecoming such a special day for us.
For both of us.
. . .
. . .
Of course the food and drink in the hall tonight are with our compliments.
. . .

Well . . .
It looked like everything was going with a swing.
Please.
Enjoy yourselves.
Thank you.

A small round of applause.
The music begins again.
Macallister *sees* **Gavin***, alone, and approaches him.*
David *sees* **Euan***, alone, and approaches him.*

Macallister   Gavin, can I . . .

Gavin   What?

Macallister   It's a tricky matter, Gavin. Can I talk to you
for a moment.

David   Euan, there you are.
If you don't mind me tearing you away from the party.
I have a job I'd like you to do for me.
It's quite important and I intend to reward you for it.
Would you come with me to the house?

They leave.
As they leave, **Euan** *sees* **Oscar** *and* **Victoria** *disappear into the*
darkness.

Macallister   Callum has stolen a revolver from the
house.
The boy has got carried away with certain ideas and . . .
I'm sure he meant no harm by it.
But you understand what could happen to him if he's
caught.
I have the revolver in my possession.
Obviously I won't show it you at the moment.
However, since you're the keeper and you've access . . .
I thought if you could take it back.
So it's never noticed missing.
Nobody need be any the wiser.
And no harm comes of it.

Gavin   Which gun's it?

Macallister *shows him.*

Gavin   Give it me.

He does.

Macallister   I have no love for the Allans, Gavin.
Or the rest of their class.
There'll be a time when we'll call for guns.
And men like you who know how to use them.
But not just yet.

Gavin   Maybe's some fights are lost already, Macallister.

Macallister   The time will come.
Just not yet.

Gavin   Keepers hold the guns.
I'll not be questioned.
I'll see it's rightly kept.

Macallister   This is very good of you, Gavin.
He's only young and it wouldn't help him to be in trouble.
I take it you won't report the incident.

Gavin   No.

14

Lord Allan *and* **Margaret**.
The wireless.
Margaret *fiddles with it. Gives up.*

Margaret   I did ask Gavin to see if he could fix it.
I thought you'd enjoy its company when we were away.
The BBC.

Lord Allan   There was a time when it would take months
for the latest news from London to reach this house.

Margaret   No need for that now.

Lord Allan   Events now speed towards us on the ether.
Events will perhaps even originate here.
Which would be a first for us.

Margaret   When we come back from Bavaria,
I intend to consider electrification in the village.
I see no reason why we should be left behind.

Lord Allan   You are aware, Margaret, that this isn't
Kent.
You haven't spent a winter here.

Margaret   I was brought up in India. I'm no stranger to
hardship.

Lord Allan   I'm sorry about my son.

Margaret   Sorry for what?

Lord Allan   Sorry for him.
Sorry.
I have no authority any longer.

Margaret   If he likes mountains he likes mountains.
I can learn to like mountains too.
Time.
As my mother said to me.
Time time time, Margaret.
There's nothing that doesn't take time and there's nothing
that time doesn't take.

Lord Allan   At least he had the sense to pick you for a
wife.
If nothing else.

Margaret   We fell in love, Lord Donald.
It's the modern way.

15

Darkness.
A red light.
A photographic darkroom.
Photos developing in a tray of chemicals.
Euan *and* **David**.

David   Euan, I asked you to come here because –
There's no history of madness in your family, is there?

Euan   No, sir.

David   Good. Good.
Euan.
I am now married and I am expected to impregnate my
wife. She is of pure racial stock. Strong-willed and with a
clear mind. She has no health problems and the women of
her family are fertile. She's likely to bear live children. But
there is a problem.
The problem, Euan, is not with one's wife it's with oneself.
She is light, Euan, and I am dark.
She's blood. I am pus.
A poison waiting to erupt.
Unfit.
So.
And I have two hundred pounds.
With what little semblance of duty I have remaining
towards history and my race,
I have gathered a pot and a pipette.

Euan   Do you want me to do something, sir?

David   I would like you to ejaculate into this pot.
This is a technique that's been used with cattle.
We can be reasonably certain of success.

Euan   You want me to wank myself into that pot?

David   For two hundred pounds.

Euan   And then what?

David   I will attempt to artificially inseminate my wife.

Euan   Will she not mind like?

David   My wife is keenly aware that my sexual behaviour is erratic, I have told her that this is the most modern method of conception. She believes the sperm is mine.
. . .
I'm aware, Euan, of how repellent I am to you.
You understand I am trying to ensure that a mistake like me doesn't happen again.

Euan   And what if she does get pregnant?

David   I'll raise the child as mine.
According to the most modern educational principles.

Euan   I might claim the child.

David   I'll make certain you don't do that.

Euan   Two hundred pounds? Show me.

David *shows him the money.*

David   I'll give it to you once the whole procedure's complete.

Euan   How'm I to do it?
The mood.
With you here, like, I can hardly take out my cock.

David   I have photographs.
These are pictures of prostitutes and other women.
I've arranged them in a small album.

Euan   Fuck's sake.

David   Be very careful how you treat this enterprise, Euan.
I chose you carefully and I've been planning for some time.
I would hate to see it spoiled.

16

The forest.
After they have had sex.
Oscar *and* **Victoria**.

Victoria   You got a cigarette?

Oscar   Aye.

He gives her a cigarette. She smokes. Coughs, she's not used to it.

Victoria   That's you bound to me, Oscar.
That's you promised.

Oscar   Not proper. Forest isn't a kirk.

Victoria   Better – it's the kirk I chose.

Oscar   No minister.

Victoria   No need of one.
There's enough ghosts here for witness.
This place knows.
You're promised me.

Oscar   Aye. Well. Promised.

Victoria   Step across that water, tomorrow.
We'll jump a train to Glasgow.
You find a boat for us.
Take it from the jetty.

Oscar   I'll find one.

Victoria   Find one now.
'Fore you sleep.
We'll meet by the tree at first light.

17

The jetty.
Euan *sitting.*
Gavin *approaches.*

Euan   Gavin?

Gavin   S'the boy here?

Euan   He's not here.
He's coming but.
In a manner of speaking.

Gavin   He's coming here?

Euan   He's to pay me.
I've done a job for him.

Gavin   I'll wait.
Drink?

Gavin *offers* **Euan** *the bottle.*
Euan *takes it.*
Euan *takes a photograph out of his pocket.*

Euan   Gav – you might want to give this back to Shona.

18

A dark room, a candle.
Victoria *packing a suitcase.*
Quietly.

19

Oscar, **Euan** *and* **Gavin**.
Gavin *has a gun.*

Oscar   Oh no.
No.
Oh fuck.

Oh fuck's sake.
You never said this, Euan.
I never said it was a murder you wanted.

Euan   We're on our way to Spain, Oscar.
Aren't we?
The police'll never catch up with us.
The boy'll not be punished unless we do it.
We can't leave it to Gavin to do it.

Oscar   Yes –
He's a cunt but –

Gavin   Worse.

Oscar   An evil cunt but –

Euan   He's a fascist, Oscar.

Oscar   An evil fascist cunt but –
fuck's sake. Murder.

Gavin   I'll do it. Go, both of you.

Euan   Oscar, this is what you have to do.
(*To* **Gavin**.) Give him the gun.

Gavin   I said I'll do it.

Euan   Oscar will do it.
You'll not be jailed, Gav.
Not right for you to suffer.
Go – go back to the ceilidh.
Before the boy comes back here.
Get yourself an alibi.

Gavin   I want to see him dead.

Euan   Go.
You'll see him dead.
Gavin.
We'll do this.
We'll do it.

Gavin *gives* **Oscar** *the gun.*
Gavin *leaves.*

Oscar   Why not you?

Euan *opens the door to the boat shed.*

Euan   Because I know I can do it.
I know I can.
But Oscar, you're all talk.
You fuck around.
You say things.
I want to know if you can do it.

David *is revealed by* **Euan***, bound and gagged.*

Oscar   Oh Jesus.
No.
No. I won't.

Euan   If not you, then who'll do it? Who'll you leave the
job to?
Gavin? Gavin'll hang for it.
We're going far away – we're going to fight in a war.

Oscar   A war but – in a war they're in the distance –

Euan   I'll do it then.
I'll take responsibility.
You go – go on – back to the village.

Oscar   I'm only saying . . .

Euan   Back to the ceilidh.
Away back to whatever lassie it is you're promised to this
time.
Go on.
You're a fucking liar.

Oscar *raises the gun.*

Oscar   Euan.

Oscar *enters the boatshed.*
A shot.
Oscar *comes out.*
He gives the gun to **Euan***.*

Euan   When we come back here, next time we see this
place.
It'll be different. It'll be ours.
Revolution's starting inside that woman.
Even now.
We'll not come back till it's finished.

20

Early morning.
Victoria *waiting at the jetty with a small suitcase.*
Gavin *enters.*

Gavin   Victoria

Victoria   Gavin.
Where is he? Where's Oscar?

Gavin   He's gone.

Victoria   Gone where?

Gavin   I don't know.
He said you'ld want took across the water.
Asked me to take you.
Said I've to give you this.

He gives her an envelope.
In it she finds a roll of two hundred pounds and a note.
She reads the note.

Victoria   Oscar.
. . .
Liar.

Gavin   You still want me to take you over the water?

Victoria   Take me over.

21

Full morning.
A tree on the lawn of the big house.
David *hanging from a butcher's hook.*
Margaret *in a nightdress.*
Lord Allan, **Mr** *and* **Mrs MacPhee**, **Mr** *and* **Mrs
Armitage**, **Mrs Wilson**.
They look but they daren't touch.

Part Two

THE CRASH

Characters

Euan, *an entrepreneur.*
Shona, *Euan's mother.*
Oscar, *Euan's father.*
Victoria, *a geologist.*
Margaret, *an elderly aristocrat.*
Jimmy, *laird of the estate.*
Norrie, *a gamekeeper.*
Bryce, *a police constable.*
Connolly, *a singer songwriter.*
Eilish, *a nurse.*
Callum, *a shopkeeper.*
Colston, *a photographer.*
McGee, *a journalist.*
Maggie, *Callum's wife.*
Carter, *an American.*

1

Dusk.
The mountainside.
A helicopter has crashed.
Carter, *an American, is trapped inside the helicopter.*

Carter Help me.
My arm is trapped.
Vicky?
I can't see.
You there?
Vicky?
My arm is trapped here.

Out of the mist and smoke emerges **Victoria**.
She is wearing a suit.
Her clothes are torn, her face dirty.

Carter There's a fire.
Vicky, please.
There's a fire starting.
I can't move the seat.
My arm is trapped.
Vicky.
Can you just help me with this?

Victoria Rock.
No lights.
No houses here.
The sea.
Carter,
This is the place.
I know this is the place.

She takes off her shoes.
She walks forward a few steps.
She sits.
She lights a cigarette.

Carter Are you still there?

Is anybody coming to get us.
Can you see anybody?

He is making an effort to free himself.

If you move this – you can move this seat –
If you could come back and –
My arm seems to be trapped by –
If you could –
Just move this –
Just –
Just –
Help.

Behind **Victoria** *the helicopter blows up.*
Light and flame.

2

Night.
The Red House.
Oscar *with* **Lady Margaret**.
Oscar *is showing plans to* **Lady Margaret**.

Oscar   This would be the library.
The classrooms. The canteen.
A theatre –
The outbuildings would be accommodation for the students.

Margaret   Who are they – these students?

Oscar   The idea is, it's for adults, for working men and
women from the islands who – want to learn.
Because people have to leave to be educated further and
perhaps this way some will be able to stay.
There's a great deal of support for the plan from the
council.

Margaret   I suppose if we say no, you're proposing to
take it from us anyway. Like they did in Russia.

Oscar   I wish it were that easy, Lady Allan.
But we propose to buy the house in the ordinary way.
I'm asking that you recognise the community's interest in
this house. In this land.
We can't necessarily afford the market rate.
But we can offer reasonably.

Margaret   Theft. Is what it amounts to.
What with the taxes and the rates – you've crippled us.
Now you've come for what's left.

Oscar   The Red House has been falling into disrepair for
some time.
You've already closed one wing of the house.
The estate makes a loss.
I'm suggesting that by selling to the community – you would
be relieving yourself of a burden.
And the community would have a resource, the people
would have a place that belonged to them.

Margaret   The people, Mr Sutherland.
You talk about them as though we don't know who they are.
They are our people.

Oscar   This house, this land has been worked by your
people for centuries. This house is not, as far as I'm
concerned – should not be yours to sell. However, the
council have discussed this and are prepared to offer you a
reasonable payment.

Margaret   What about the work this family has put in –
Keeping this house alive.
Looking after it.
Does that carry any weight?
Will they teach that at your college?

Oscar   Our college.
You would be able to use the facilities, just like anyone else.
I've asked the council to make you a formal offer.
I hope you'll consider it.

Jimmy *enters with a bottle of wine and some glasses.*

Margaret It isn't up to me to consider, ultimately.
The future of this house rests with my son.

Jimmy In which case the place is condemned.
Drop of claret, Oscar?

Oscar No thank you.

Jimmy It's old. Found it at the back of the cellar.
(*Looks at the date.*)
Been here as long as I have.
(*Tastes it.*)
Aged rather more gracefully, however.

Oscar You've seen this proposal, Lord Allan.
Have you given it any thought?

Jimmy The Red House full of students.
I quite like the idea.
A bit of life.
I can't help wondering what my father would have made of
it.
You know, he was very interested in education.
He was something of a radical.

Oscar I'm sure he would have approved.

Margaret What Jimmy's saying is we'll consider your
proposal.

Jimmy That's what I'm saying.

Margaret But we're by no means decided to sell.
To the council or to anyone else.

3

Night.
A council house.
Shona *and* **Euan**.
Euan *has finished eating.*
A new, portable, television is on the table.

Euan   That was good soup.
Your soup, You should do B and B, Mum.
There's money in that scene.
Tourists.
I was driving over the causeway this evening
and I thought –
Mountains, sea, forest.
You've got the whole shebang here.
You should think about it.

Shona   It's very wee.

Euan   Japanese.
This is the very latest thing.

Shona   Oscar won't have a television in the house.
Says it's all propoganda.

Euan   Keep it in the shed if you want.
It's a present.

Shona   I've always fancied watching television myself.
See what's on.
See what they're up to.
He watches it the pub, you know.

Euan   Let's get it plugged in.

Shona   S'not propaganda when it's in the pub.

Euan *plugs the television in and starts trying to find reception.*

Euan   Takes a minute to find the channel.

Shona   Will you be staying, Euan?
We don't see you much.

Euan   I don't know.
I'm here till Connolly writes some decent songs.
Said the country air would do him good.
Get him away from temptation.
No temptation here.
Money he's spends.
Lazy bastard's taking me to the brink.

We should get a picture in a minute.
Where is dad, anyway?

Shona   He's up at the Red House.
He's trying to get the council to buy it.

Euan (*nearly gets something*)   Here we go – shite.
The council? What?

Shona   To make a college of it.

Euan   The council. Christ's sakes.

Shona   Maybe it's broken.

Euan   It's not broken.

Shona   He's got big plans. Since he's been elected he's
been working away. Just hear him talk about it. He talks.

Euan   The council.
You should see America. There's none of this council crap
in America, I'm telling you. In Glasgow there's rubbish
lying in the streets, strikes everywhere – folk sat on their
arses all day moaning like janitors. We're a nation of bloody
janitors.
None of that in America.
Scotland is nowhere. Nowhere in any league. .
This is the council for you.
Shoot the lot of them.

Shona *is looking at a newspaper.*

Euan   What's on?

Shona   *The Generation Game.*

Euan   We'll get it in a minute.

Shona and **Euan** *both look at the telly broadcasting snow.*

Shona   He's very funny.
That chappie.
The one who does it.
I've seen it.
Maybe it needs to be bigger to work.

Euan   This television is state-of-the-art.
This television is –
Sitting waiting to broadcast to you
Pin-sharp pictures.
Like real.
And we can't even get reception for Christ's sake.
People should be up in arms about it.

Oscar *enters from outside.*
A moment.

Euan   It's a present.

Oscar   Didn't know you were coming.
You never said he was coming, Shona.

Euan   Not staying long.

Shona   He's bought us a television.
It doesn't work.

Euan   It works, it's just the reception.

Oscar   It's as well you're here.
You'll need to come with me.
Put your coat on – we're going up the hill.

Shona   It's late for walking, Oscar.

Oscar   There's been a crash.
Aeroplane, something, helicopter
Crashed on the hill.
Gordie Bryce wants volunteers.

Shona   A plane crash?

Oscar   C'mon, we'll go now.

Shona   Maybes we'll see something about it on the news.

Oscar *and* **Euan** *exit.*

Shona *looks at the telly.*

4

Day.
The mountainside.
An arrangement on the ground of broken open suitcases and other
personal effects.
Norrie, **Callum**, *and* **Constable Bryce**.

Bryce   When you find something, Norrie, mark where
you found it on the map. Then you put a label on the item.
So if it's personal belongings, you mark it P, then NM,
which is your code. Callum, you're CR, then one, two,
three, whatever for each one you find.
If it's wreckage the code's A.
And if it's a body, or a piece of a body, the code's HR.

Norrie   When you see this. Some guy's razor. He'd have
been having this morning.

Callum   Maybe he'd have been hung-over.
Maybes from drinking at his hotel.

Norrie   Scotch. On the rocks. Isn't that what the
Americans call it?

Callum   Were they all Americans?

Bryce   All but the pilot.
It was a charter out of Aberdeen.

Callum   There's stuff all over the hill.
Seen pieces half a mile down, round by the corrie.
Seen a shoe just off the forest road.
Didn't know if it was some guy's shoe from the crash, or if it
had always been there and I'd just never noticed it before.

Bryce   Mark it anyway.
Forensic boys want it all marked.
We'll need all the men we can get to gather it.

Norrie   I called the keepers from Aultbhea and the
lighthouse.
Said they'd come.

Bryce   This is a big thing for me.

These poor bastards land here.

Folk'll want to know why.

So we need to collect everything. Every small thing.

They'll be thinking maybe we can't handle an operation like this.

But it was our mountain they hit.

So it's our job.

Norrie   Taking bodies down last night. Me and some of the Inverness boys. Took them on stretchers as far as the hill road then in the back of the Land Rover to the village. Just at dawn, sun's rising over the loch, Inverness boy says, 'Beautiful part of the world this, never been up this way before.' I said to Eilish, after – the place you'll end up dead in.

You don't know it.

But it maybe waits for you.

5

A small bedroom.
Daylight, the curtains closed.
Victoria *asleep in bed.*
Oscar, **Euan** *and* **Shona** *around the bed.*

Shona   She's bonny.

To have been in a crash.

You wouldn't know.

She'll not want to wake up alone.

Oscar   She'll be tired.

Euan   She's strong. Strong enough to walk last night.
We nearly didn't find her.

Oscar   She was quiet.

Euan   She'd walked that far from the wreck we nearly missed her.

But I caught her face in the torchlight.

I was looking.
I saw her sat on a stone.
Her eyes were open.
She was looking straight at me.

Oscar   She'll need to go to hospital.
Be properly seen.

Shona   She'll be tired to travel.
Doctor can come here.

Euan   I'll sleep on the couch.

Shona   Do her people know she's with us?

Oscar   She'll want seen by someone.

Shona   She'll maybe want to use our telephone.

Euan   She's American, she told me.
She asked where she was.
And I said Scotland.
And she said –
'Where exactly?' – 'Where exactly?' she said.

Shona   Our hill she hit.
Seems right that we're to look after her.

Oscar   There are procedures now, procedures.
We'll need to inform whichever of the authorities need
informing.
She'll need to be seen.

Shona   Shh.

Victoria *is waking up.*
They watch.
She wakes up.
She sits up in bed.
A moment.

Victoria   I remember you.
Your light.
From the mountain.
You found me.

Shona   Euan took you down from the hill.
Last night.

Victoria   Euan.
I remember.

Shona   I'm Shona, Euan's mother, this is my husband,
Oscar.
This is our house.

Victoria   I remember.

Shona   Are you comfortable?

Victoria   I'm OK.

Euan   OK. She says – you hear that.
After what she's been through.
OK.
OK.

Oscar   What's your name, lass?

Shona   She doesn't want questions, Oscar.

Oscar   Just so her people know she's here.

Victoria   Victoria.

Oscar   Victoria.

Victoria   I like Vicky better.

Euan   Vicky.

Oscar   Where do you come from, Victoria, in America?

Victoria   I come from Illinois.

Oscar   Illinois.

Euan   Illinois.

Shona   Illinois.

Oscar   We've taken you in, just for now, Victoria.

Shona   She'll be hungry.

Oscar   Just for now.
Till you've been seen.
Then you can go
– home.

Victoria   Home?

Oscar   To Illinois.

Victoria   Of course.
I have to go back.

Euan   You don't have to go.
You can stay as long as you want.
This is my room.
What you've been through.

Shona   Would you like something to eat?
Soup.
A cup of tea.

Euan   What it must have been like.
What was it like?

Oscar   She'll not want to talk about it.

Victoria   Have you got coffee?

Shona   We don't have coffee.
We have tea.

Oscar   Euan – away down to Maggie's – see if she's got
coffee.

Victoria   Tea's OK.

Euan   I want coffee.
I might have a cup of coffee myself.
I'll arrange for a cup.

Victoria   You're very kind.
I should pay you for your trouble.
I have insurance.

Shona   You can't pay us.

Victoria   But if a doctor's coming?

Oscar   We don't pay for doctors here.
You've no need to think of money.

Euan   If there's anything you want – just ask me.
I can get hold of – whatever – whatever you might want.
I'll make arrangements.
Just ask.

Victoria   Is it day?
What time is it?
I'll open these curtains.

She starts to get out of bed.
She stands.
Oscar *and* **Euan** *get up.*
Oscar *holds her arm.*

Victoria   I'm OK.

Oscar *lets go of her arm.*
She walks to the window.
She opens the curtains.

Victoria   I remember.
Mountains. Sea. Forest.
Is the water deep?

Oscar   Deep enough.
Lucky it wasn't the water you hit.

Victoria   When I walked out last night,
Out of the fire,
There were no lights – no houses.
But I recognised this place.
I recognised it straightaway.

6

In **Norrie** *and* **Eilish***'s garden.*
Connolly *hunched over a guitar, strumming.*

Connolly   'Like an aircrash.
You love me like an aircrash, baby.'

Pause.

Connolly   'Where were you?
Where were you?
When that big bird came down.
Where were you?'

Eilish *enters wearing a nurse's uniform.*

Eilish   Mr Connolly. That's your breakfast ready for you.

Connolly   Eilish. I didn't expect to see you this morning.
You must be tired after last night.

Eilish   Not too bad.
I've to go into hospital but.
It'll only go cold. So you're as well to eat it now.

Connolly   You've made me breakfast.
After a night with no sleep.

Eilish   It's no trouble, Mr Connolly.

Connolly   Eilish, you can call me Dan.
I could have made my own breakfast.

Eilish   Well, it's done now.

Connolly   You know what, Eilish.
I've a good feeling here – positive.
This grounds me. You ground me.
Country food. Country weather.
Positive.
Sit with me, inspire me before you go.

Eilish   I'm a bit late for work.

Connolly   Sit with me.

Eilish   I suppose I could. Hospital' not miss me.
They're all dead.
Not much I can do.

She sits.

Connolly   I'm writing a song.
Touring, hotels, I haven't written a note.
Here, with you looking after me,
I feel connected.

Eilish   You've been to America, haven't you?

Connolly   All the time.

Eilish   I want to go to America.

Connolly   America's OK. Euan wanted me to record in
America.
But you know – it moves too fast –
I said to Euan – take me to somewhere that doesn't move so
fast. Take me to a different time zone.
He took me here.

Eilish   Aye, well.
It's a different time zone here, right enough.
Clock's stopped.

Connolly   I'll take you to America.
You can come to a gig.
Euan can arrange it.

Eilish   What I want and what happens – not the same
thing.

Connolly   I'll take you to New York.
You help me write.
You can inspire me.

Eilish   Well – your breakfast'll go cold if you don't eat it so.

Connolly   I'll talk to Euan.
Leave it with me.

Eilish *goes to leave.*

Eilish   How long are you meaning to stay here, Dan?

Connolly   Y'in a hurry for me to leave, Eilish?

Eilish   Didn't say that.

Connolly   I don't know.
Feels like home already.
They tell me in the pub that big red house is for sale.
Maybe I'll buy the place.
So we can be neighbours.
I can eat your cooking every day.

7

The Red House.
The room with the modern chair and the wireless.
Jimmy *searching through books.*
Noting, writing.
Margaret *enters from outside.*

Margaret   I wanted Norrie to start painting the
boathouse today but he's nowhere to be found.
I rang his house. No answer.
The wood's rotting. It'll fall into the loch.

Jimmy   He's with the men on the hill. Looking for
wreckage.

Margaret   You should be with them.
Working.

Jimmy   This is work.

Margaret   Apparently several Americans have died.
That strikes me as considerably more important than
whatever questionable book you're reading.
I thought these had been thrown out.

Jimmy   I found them.

Margaret   You should be out there – involved.

Jimmy   They know the hill.

Margaret   You should know the hill.

Jimmy   I should.
I'm ashamed.

Margaret   You should know the hill from stalking.
If you had ever been stalking you would – perhaps be useful
now.

She sits in the modern chair.

Your grandfather would have attended an incident like
this.
Your grandfather would have been at the centre of things.
Lending authority.

Jimmy   Other people have authority. The police. The
council. It's really none of our business.

Margaret   Council, everything's council.
The council and their petty little caretakers.
I saw them coming over the causeway this morning.
A line of cars with their lights flashing.
Suddenly we're the centre of attention.
We're the landowners, Jimmy.

Jimmy   Not for much longer, I hope.
There's another buyer coming round this afternoon.
To have a look at the house.

Margaret   – you're still an Allan
However louche you affect to be about your position,
Jimmy, your name still means something in this place.
I think you should intervene.

8

Victoria *at the window.*
Euan *enters with a mug.*

Euan   This is instant coffee. This saves time. We have a kettle – just here. And I brought you a mug. You can pour the hot water straight on to the coffee. It's freeze-dried. The water remakes it. Of all the types of instant coffee I've tried, this one is the best.

Victoria   We have this in America too.

Euan   Of course you do. You'll be used to it.
Here.
. . .
And if you want use the phone,
I've set it up on the landing so you can use it.
I'll get it.
I'll bring it to you.

He brings on a phone, the wire doesn't quite reach her chair.
He tries to make it stretch.
He puts it on the floor.
She drinks.

Euan   The view – mountains, sea, forest – the whole shebang.

Victoria   Empty.
Who does it belong to?
This land?

Euan   All belongs to the estate.

Victoria   This coffee tastes weird.

Euan   It's the water. Maybe the water. It comes straight off the hill.

Victoria   Granite.

Euan   What?

Victoria   The hills.
Granite – volcanic.
I'm a geologist.

Euan   A geologist – I thought –

Victoria   What?

Euan   To be truthful, I thought you were a stewardess.
A geologist – that's rocks.

Victoria   Rocks and time.
I work for oil companies.
I read the landscape for them.

Euan   Oil's over the east coast.
There's no oil here –
Is there?

Victoria   It was my first trip out.
It wasn't oil exactly we were looking for.
It doesn't matter now.
Does it?

Euan   No.
I suppose.
Well.
I'll let you – if you want anything.

Euan *goes to leave.*
She looks at the phone.

Victoria   Everyone else is dead.
No one's told me.
Are they dead?

Euan   Yes.
Were they your – collegues?

Victoria   My boss. My collegues. Some others. I never
met them before.

Euan   It must be – I can't imagine –

Victoria   I should phone the company – I should make
contact.
I should go back.

Euan   The phone's there – you can use it any time.
Long distance. Anything.
I'll arrange it.

Victoria   Thank you.

He leaves.
She picks up the phone, dials,
Stretches the flex so she is back at the window.
She stops.
She puts the phone down.

9

The police station.
Oscar *and* **Constable Bryce**.
A map with pins in it.
Bryce *taking notes.*

Bryce   Can you show me exactly where you were at the
impact moment?

Oscar   Here.

Bryce   I will code you OS and your statement is number
seven.
So, you've said that you were in the hall, at a council
meeting when you all heard a sound . . .
Can you describe the sound for me?

Oscar   It was very like the sound of artillery fire.
Outgoing artillery.

Bryce   You can't think of any other words . . .

Oscar   That's what it sounded like.

Bryce   What does outgoing artillery fire sound like?
I've never heard that sound.

Oscar   It sounds like boots in new snow.
It can be a pleasant sound.
Because it's far away from you.

Bryce   So, what? a crunching sound? Can I put that
down?

Oscar   No. It's not like crunching toast, or gravel, say.
It's softer. The earth takes the force of the explosion.

Bryce   Is it like a 'crump'?

Oscar   What?

Bryce   You know in comics the artillery goes 'crump.'
C.R.U.M.P.
That's the word.
The man throws a grenade into a bunker.
Crump.

Oscar   It has nothing to do with comics.

Bryce   No, I know, Oscar, but . . . I have to . . .
My report needs to be clear.

Oscar   I've seen these comics you're talking about.
They're innacurate . . .
. . .
War has no 'crump' sound in it. No sounds of that type.
I know the sound I'm talking about.
The sound of metal tearing up earth.

Bryce   The sound of metal tearing up earth.

Oscar   And fire.

Bryce   And fire.

Oscar   And things being torn open.

Bryce   Torn open.
Thank you, Oscar.
These are clues. They have no meaning for us, of
course.

We don't have the wider picture.
But to the investigator, they're clues to the cause of the
crash.

10

The mountainside.
Euan *and* **Norrie**.
The gathering of wreckage and belongings.
Norrie *in working clothes.* **Euan** *in his suit.* **Euan** *is examining a watch in a clear plastic bag. He takes out some cigarettes.*

Euan   This watch.
Do you know how much this watch is worth?
This is a fine watch.

Norrie   No use to the guy now.

Euan   You saying I should steal it?

Norrie   No.

Euan   This watch gives me respect for the dead guy.
He earned this some way.
I'm not stealing his watch.

Norrie   I'm just saying. It's a shame.

Euan   Do you remember coming up here to smoke, when we were kids?

Norrie   Aye.

Euan   God, I was after Eilish then.

Norrie   Aye, well.

Euan   I tried to get my hand in her jumper once and she hit me.
Did she ever tell you that?

Norrie   Aye. She told me that right enough.

Euan   The girls when we were that age, Norrie, Christ . . .

So fucking fresh, you know.
So fucking tight in their jumpers.
So fucking beautiful.
You have to hold on to those pictures, you know.
Remember what you wanted when you were a raw kid.
That gives you power.

Norrie   See in the night, Euan.
I was taking the bodies down off the hill.

Euan   Nightmare. No doubts.

Norrie   It made me think, Euan.

Euan   It would.

Norrie   Because – I'm sick of this hill, Euan, taking dead
things off it.
So where am I going?

Euan   Norrie, that's a question everyone's got to ask
themselves.
Where am I going?

Norrie   Euan, I'm not in a crash, like these guys.
That's not what I'm saying.
But I feel like I'm sinking, Euan.
The situation I'm in. I'm sinking into it awful slowly.

Euan   You can change that. You can turn that around.

Norrie   You're doing well enough, though, aren't you?

Euan   I do OK.

Norrie   You're making money, like.

Euan   I work for it.

Norrie   I know that.

Euan   I'm on the phone. I'm in the office.

Norrie   Connolly, though, he's a star, he's doing well for
you.

Euan   Connolly was a rich seam. I saw him in a club. I saw – potential. Mined the potential. But that seam is very close to exhaustion. I'm still looking.

Norrie   But you'll find something. Because you're a success.

Euan   I don't sit.
Everyone sits around on their arse waiting.
But not me, Norrie.
I've been to America.

Norrie   Eilish wants to go to America.

Euan   See, in America people don't look at things and say . . .
I don't know . . . there's rain, or there's a sunset, or there's a person who's crying.

Norrie   No?

Euan   No. In America they've trained themselves to see the opening.
So they say, there's rain, I'll sell umbrellas.
Or there's a sunset, I'll take a photo for a calendar,
There's a person crying, I'll sell them a hanky.
They move into the opening.

Norrie   I was thinking, Euan, you might be . . .
. . .
What with Eilish wanting to go and –
and, you coming back, and me feeling this –
I'm wondering about making a break, you know.
A new start.
Because I don't make money, Euan.
We get by but . . . it's not a life where you can see ahead of yourself.
And I was thinking about maybe asking you if you needed anything done?

Euan   What sort of thing?

Norrie   Well, in the showbusiness management field. You know that's not very much my area but I'm sure there's something I could do . . .

Euan   You're thinking of setting up . . .

Norrie   I'm asking you if you've got a job.

Euan   Norrie. What in fuck's name are you about?

Norrie   I'm asking you . . .

Euan   Fuck's sake, Norrie.
You ask me to come up the hill with you.
I'm thinking this is an old times' scene.
Don't ask me for a job.
You're my friend.
Jesus, Norrie.

Norrie   I'm asking because you're my friend.

Euan   If I have a job I advertise it, Norrie.
Apply.
I can't believe you asked me that.
If you're the right person you get the job.
I'm trying not to be hard on you here.
You've had a deep encounter with death, but Norrie, Jesus . . .
You've put me in a position.
I'm trying to be clear.
I make money, Norrie.
I can't pull folk up with me.

Norrie   I thought it was a fair enough question.

Euan   Well, it wasn't, Norrie.

Norrie   Aye, well.

Euan   I'm sorry.
I went mental there on you.
You're a pal.
Only, Norrie, we punish success in this country and it boils me up, man. I own a Ferrari. You buy a Ferrari because you want to drive fast, alone or with a pretty girl in the

bucket seat beside you, skirt riding round her hips. If you
want to take the whole fucking village along for the ride you
buy a fucking bus. I'm into Ferraris, Norrie. That's all I'm
saying. Respect that, man. You know . . . wave to me as I
drive past.
. . .
I'll see what I can do for you.

11

The Red House.
Connolly, **Jimmy** *and* **Margaret**.

Connolly   I love this place.
I know this place.
I've known it. The curtains are heavy . . . the way they hang
there.
I recognise it. Studio here, communal kitchen there,
vegetable gardens . . .
It's as if I've had dreams about this place without actually
ever being here. It's fantastic.
You can actually touch the history.

Margaret   This isn't just an old house, you know, Mr
Connolly.
This is a working house.

Connolly   That's clear. You can sense that.
. . .
Imagine this room full of beanbags . . .
Just . . . everywhere, a big soft room . . .
Relax, open the curtains, watch the sea changing colours . . .
This place is buried in my subconscious, Lady Margaret,
you know, and just standing here, it's all bubbling up.
Do you believe in reincarnation, Lady Margaret?

Margaret   I'm afraid not, Mr Connolly.

Connolly   I don't know if I do either.
Too many weird questions.

But if I did, this would be the place to convince me, this house.

Jimmy   I believe in reincarnation.

Margaret   Jimmy studies these things. In an academic way.

Jimmy   My father was very interested in Hinduism.
He died before I was born.
I've been investigating his life.

Connolly   The Bhagwan, all that stuff?

Jimmy   The Vedic scriptures. He left a collection.

Connolly   I'd love to see that collection, Jimmy,
I'd like to connect with that wisdom.

Jimmy   We haven't decided to sell to a private buyer.
There is interest from the council.
If we were to sell to you we'd have to make certain stipulations.
I don't think we could allow structural change, for example.

Connolly   The structure's fine. No change required, Lord A, this is an ancient structure. Only a fool disturbs an ancient structure. There are ancestors to consider.

Jimmy   There's the matter of access. This house was visited by Boswell and Johnson. Historians, I mean, literary historians for example, might want to see it from time to time . . .

Margaret   What Jimmy's talking about is very hypothetical.
Because we're by no means decided to sell.

Connolly   What kind of money is this?
I need to ask my manager.
I'm just dreaming.
I don't know if I've got this kind of money.

Margaret   I don't want to discuss this any more. I'm afraid.
Jimmy and I have plenty of work to be getting on with.
Perhaps if you write to our lawyer with your ideas we would give them our consideration.
As I said before, this is a working house.
This is our office as well as our home.

Jimmy   If you're interested in the Vedas, Mr Connolly, I could show you the library, I'm cataloguing the collection.

Connolly   Lord A, I would love to see that – library – inspiration.

Margaret   So if you'll excuse me.
Jimmy?

Jimmy   Oh. Yes.
Come on. I'll take you up.

Connolly   It's been a pleasure to meet you, Lady M.

Margaret   I'm sure it has.

Connolly   Whao.
This door.
I've turned towards this door.
In some crazy circumstances.
That was definitely a déjà vu.

12

The police station.
Maggie, **Callum** *and* **Constable Bryce**.
Bryce *is examining an expensive black attaché case.*

Bryce   It's good you brought this in, Callum.

Maggie   It must be made well to not be broken more.

Callum   It was half into the bog. Where it landed. The bog cushioned it.

Bryce   Because it must belong to somebody. Somebody dead.

Callum   Is it leather, Gordie? The covering?

Bryce   It feels like leather.

Maggie   Some plastic feels like leather, mind you.

Bryce   Leather but metal underneath.

Maggie   It's a metal casing.

Callum   Leather and metal, there's something important in that case.

Bryce   You might be right.

Maggie   The man that was the owner of that case, before he died, was some kind of a big shot.

Callum   No doubt.

Maggie   The man that was the owner of that case was not travelling on holiday.

Callum   He wasn't coming for the golf.

Maggie   He was on some type of business.

Bryce   We don't know that.

Maggie   To my mind there's only one business.

Callum   Do you think it might be some type of illegal activities?

Bryce   Now you're making allegations.
We have no evidence.

Maggie   I'm surprised it wasn't handcuffed to the man's hand.
We could have had a hand attached to this thing.

Callum   Oh God.

Maggie   I've a feeling it's oil.

Callum   A tycoon?

Bryce   There's oil men hanging round in Inverness right enough.

Callum   There's that many of them.
They're all over.
Donald up at Garve's saying they're looking round here.

Bryce   Looking for oil?

Callum   Scouting – prospecting – they're looking for places to build the rigs.

Maggie   Have you ever seen those rigs?

Bryce   Only on television.

Maggie   They're the size of skyscrapers.

Callum   It takes ten boats to tow them out to the oil fields.
The engineering in a project like that.
Very impressive.

Maggie   There's a fair kind of money in oil. That's one thing you can be sure of.

Bryce   Donald up at Garve says they're looking round here?

Callum   That's what he says.

Bryce   Metal and leather, safety-locking devices . . .

Callum   Give it a shake. See what's in it.

Bryce *raises the briefcase to shake it.*

Maggie   Don't shake it, it could be a bloody bomb.

Bryce *shakes the briefcase.*

Maggie   Paper.

Callum   Money maybe?

Maggie   Are you going to open it?

Callum   You'ld have to break it if you were going to open it.

Bryce   You were right to bring it in, Maggie. But I can't break open the property of dead people.

Callum   But you'll not know who it belongs to unless you see what's in it.

Bryce   There are the proper channels for these things, Callum.

Maggie   Gordie, you are the proper channels.

Callum   That's leather and metal, Gordie, with a special code to unlock it. You're the only person with the proper authority to open up a thing like that.

Maggie   The Inverness boys'll want to see it.

Callum   You're the man on the spot, Gordie.

Bryce   I am the investigating officer.

Callum   There might be clues in it, for your investigations.

Maggie   Even if it's just to give it back to the man's wife, poor woman, you'll want to open it for that alone.

Callum   The Inverness boys'll only open it themselves.

Bryce   You might be right.

Callum   Give me a hold of it.

He holds it.

You would need a hacksaw.

Maggie   At the very least.

Callum   Maybe a crowbar.

Bryce   If I'm going to open this I'm going to want to do it cleanly.

Maggie   Disturb it as little as possible.

Bryce   Give it here.

He takes the case and goes off.

Pause.

Maggie   He shouldn't open that thing.

Callum   I'm not sure a constable has the authority to open a thing like that.

Maggie   He'll be heading for trouble.

Callum   The man can't satisfy his curiosity. That's his trouble.

Maggie   It's a Pandora's box.

Callum   It's a very dangerous Pandora's box.

A shotgun fired nearby.

Maggie   That's it done.

Callum   Can't be undone now.

13

Amongst boxes of books, **Connolly** *and* **Jimmy** *smoking a joint.*
Connolly *looking at the books.*

Connolly   This stuff, Jimmy, this is – a gold mine. Does this stuff come with the house?

Jimmy   I'm taking it with me to India, I'm afraid.

Connolly   To India?

Jimmy   I'm writing a book about my father's work. Some of the thinking I've found – it's powerful.
He was pushing the limits, exploring – thinking about nature –about life – you know – he was a rebel – I've inherited that.

Connolly   I've been to India – Kashmir –

Always looking for inspiration.
Looking for a guru – you know.
Looking –

Jimmy   Everyone's looking now – for some way to
connect with something greater than ourselves – with
nature. He was ahead of his time – this is what I'm finding
out.

Connolly   I was in an airport, red seats in rows facing
each other, and it was like the seats at we used to have at
school. An aeroplane was called, I was carried to another
city, I'm introduced to another audience – the cameras
swung around me – and suddenly I was somewhere else
again. When I was a scaffolder in Dundee we used to swing
the scaffolding from hand to hand, it never fell.
The cameras swung around me and I sang the song.
But I was somewhere else.
I'm looking for something that connects.

Jimmy   There is connection, and there's no connection.
This is what the Vedas teach.

Connolly   Right.
. . .
You gonnae explain that?

Jimmy   There are four ages, in history.
Each age is a decline on the previous.
In the first age everything that needs to be done, is done.
All men are good.
In the second age, men discover motivation, reward and
punishment.
And have become corrupted.
In the third age,
Disunity prevails, difference emerges, and catastrophe
begins.
In the last age, the age in which we're living,
Evil has become triumphant.
Civilisation recedes.

Marriage takes place between castes, women go with
worthless men, blood ties disintegrate, commerce governs all
meaning,
In due course time itself falls towards destruction.
Then there is rebirth, and the cycle begins again.
Each cycle, which lasts four million years, is one minute
of one day in the life of Brahman. Brahman lives for a
hundred years. When Brahman dies, the universe is reborn.
Everything is contained within the cycle of time.
The connection is in time.

14

Oscar *playing his fiddle at the table.*
There is a bottle of whisky and a glass in front of him.
Euan *is trying to sleep on the couch, covered in a blanket.*

Oscar   You don't mind me playing.

Euan   No. No.

Euan *puts a cushion over his head.*
Oscar *plays a moment more.*

Oscar   I'll stop if you want.

Euan   It's your house. You play.

Oscar   You should make a record of this.
You could make a lot of money.
Out of real music.

Euan   Folk's out.
Glam's in.
Whatever you are, Father.
You're not glam.

Oscar   And I suppose you are.
Your world is glamorous.
Jet set.

Euan   Not at this precise moment, no.

Oscar   To go to America is glamorous.
Not here.
Not to be among ordinary folk.
Working.

Euan   I work.

Oscar   For yourself.

Euan   You don't change, do you.
Same tune.
Crack in the vinyl.
Over and over.
Meanwhile, this place's sliding off the map.
You're all talk.

Oscar   In the village they're saying – if they've found oil, offshore,
It'll mean work.
Proper work.
You could come back – you could involve yourself.

Victoria *has entered.*
She is wearing a man's dressing gown.

Euan   Takes Americans to find what's under our own water.
Scots sat and nobody looked.
Rock and sea's all we saw.
We didn't see the opening.
They saw – they moved – that's the difference.

Oscar   If we were governed right, it'd be used right.

Euan   If the Americans are coming we should be thinking – what's the opening? What do they need? They've found oil – what do they need?
I've been racking my brains for it.

Oscar   All that time it was under there.
We didn't know.
Oil.

Victoria   It's everywhere.
We'll all become it.
Depending on where our bodies lie in the rock,
we'll all turn into oil or coal or gas.
Something that burns.
– the men I worked with –
They'll become what they were looking for.
Atoms underground. Somewhere.
I was awake.
I heard you playing.

Oscar   I'm sorry.
We didn't mean to disturb you.

Victoria   Do you have a cigarette?

Euan   Here.

He gives her a cigarette. Lights it.
She coughs.
She sits down.

Victoria   Never smoked before.
Now I want to.

Oscar   I shouldn't smoke.
Always have.
American cigarettes.
American – like you.
Sit down. Sit here.

Euan   Pour her a drink, Dad.
You want a drink?
I'm having one.
I was just about to have one.

Oscar *pours a drink for them both.*

Victoria   I can't seem to sleep anyway.
Every time I close my eyes.
I see the crash.

Oscar   It passes.
Those pictures go.

Victoria   Do they?

Oscar   I was in the war.
When I came home, I still saw things, heard voices.

Victoria   Do you see them now?

Oscar   Not so often.

Victoria   We were talking about TV.
About Mary Tyler Moore.
Do you get that show?

Euan   Not here. There's no reception here.

Victoria   We were in the middle of talking and then it
went dark.
I felt the floor pull away from me.
The floor fell.
I seemed to have no weight.
Not falling, not flying.
I remember having time to think.
Must have been seconds, microseconds.
But I had time to think.
This is what it's like.
This is what this experience is like.

Euan   I've had that feeling.
Not in a crash.
In a different way.

Victoria   Then it hit.
Things thrown around – seats – bags – bottles, nothing
where it should be. Everything was everywhere. Moving.
Hours to think.
To watch.

Euan   When Connolly went to number one in the charts,
I had that same feeling.
In a different way.

Victoria   Then it was quiet.
I climbed through the hatch.
I felt coldness and dark and wet.

I saw no lights.
I kicked off my shoes and felt the wet through my
stockings.
Carter, my boss,
His arm was stuck between two seats.
He shouted –
He was calling to me.
But he couldn't move.
He wanted me to go back –
To help him but –

Euan   He must have been a freezer.
They say – scientists – that the world divides into those who
freeze and those who move.
I read that recently.

Victoria   I wasn't afraid then.
I walked away.
I'm afraid now.

Oscar   Maybe you couldn't have saved him.
You can't save everybody.

Victoria   I don't know.
I didn't try.
Should I have tried?

Euan   You survived because you wanted to live.

Victoria   I felt relaxed.
I felt as though I was walking – in a new body.
Empty.

Oscar   Some people survive for no reason.
Chance.
We do our best for each other in the face of chance.

She closes her eyes.
Oscar *holds her hand.*

Victoria   I can see the fire.
I can hear him.

She opens her eyes.

I've always been afraid of an atomic bomb.
I used to imagine what it might be like.
And I used to think – where would I be, what would I be
doing when it happened. Would I be in my apartment?
Would I be scared? Would I survive? Would I want to
survive?
But after the crash, looking out of your window. I realised –
this place – the Atlantic and these mountains and clouds
that seem – like blankets. Being here I thought – this is what
I imagined. This is what the world was like before and
maybe this is the world after. After the fire.

Shona *has entered.*
She stands.

Shona   You'll be wanting to go home soon, I suppose,
now you're on your feet.
To America.

Victoria   Do you want me to go?

Oscar   You can stay as long as you want.

Shona   You two – keeping her awake.
You should be ashamed of yourselves.
It's late, Oscar.

Victoria   The music you were playing – I liked it.

Oscar   It's just an old tune.

Victoria   Is it a Scottish tune?

Oscar   It's a tune.

Victoria   Does it have a name?

Oscar   No.
Not that I remember.

Shona   Are you coming, Oscar?
Leave the lassie in peace.

Oscar   Aye, I'm coming.
Good night.

Shona   Good night.

Shona *and* **Oscar** *leave.*
Euan *sits with* **Victoria**.

Victoria   I won't go back, Euan.
I'm going to call the company.
Tell them I'm leaving my job.
That apartment, that job, that – fear I had.
That way of living.
That world burned.
Illinois burned.
I walked away.

Euan   You're alive because you saw life and you had the
strength to move.
That's what you're saying.

He holds her hand – not noticing he is doing it.

Peripheral vision – I believe this – we evolved to see animals
moving. In a still forest it's the bird rising from the tree that
we see. In the savannah it's the moving leopard. We see
movement from the corners of our eyes.
And we attack. That's what you did. You operated on an
unconscious level.

Victoria   What about you?
What level do you operate on?

Euan *hesitates.*
He goes to kiss her.
Hesitates again.
Kisses her.
She kisses back.
They stop.

Euan   He didn't move.
I did.

Victoria   I know what they need.

Euan   Who?

Victoria   The company.
I know.
I know.

15

Callum, **Colston** *and* **McGee** *by the tree, on the road.*

Colston   Callum, could you just . . .
Nearer the tree . . . yeah, yeah, could you point with your
hand . . .

Callum   What do you want me to point to?

Colston   Just point.
Like you're pointing at something important.
Great. Great. Terrific.

McGee   Callum, what did you say your job was?

Callum   I do some work for the estate, you know . . . and
. . .
I run a bed and breakfast establishment.

McGee   So you're a gamekeeper. What age are you,
Callum?

Colston   Look up.

Callum   I'm fifty-four.

Colston   Lovely. Callum, see you're looking straight into
the camera.
That's good but now I want you to look towards the village.
OK?

McGee   Callum, I've got what you told me about the
crash.
Discovering the wreckage, the darkness, the cries in the
darkness, which is good. What I'm looking for now is the
background.
How do you think something like this will affect the village?

Callum I don't know. It hasn't happened before.

McGee Will the village recover?

Callum From what?

McGee From the shock.

Callum Oh. Aye.

Colston OK. Callum . . . that's great. Can you just turn towards me.
And look down, that's it.

Callum Do you still want me to point?

Colston No. You can stop pointing.

McGee What's the significance of a thing like this, Callum?
What does it mean, to a small community?

Callum I don't know. I'm sorry.

Colston Callum, you're smiling at me.

Callum Do you not want me to smile?

Colston I want you to look sad.

Callum Sad? What about?

Colston Well, maybe not sad. Regretful, you know, sombre.

Callum OK.

McGee In the long run. Will the crash change anything in the village?

Colston You're still smiling.

Callum I'm not.

Colston You are.

Callum This is just the way my face is.

Colston   The thing is, a picture, if you're smiling in it we can't use it.
Because what we're illustrating here is a tragedy.

Callum   It's my face.

Colston   OK. Just think about a bad thing, you know.
Think about if it was a friend of yours on the helicopter, say.

Callum   OK. I'm imagining that.
. . .

McGee   So can you tell me about the way the crash will affect the village?

Callum   It might help with the tourists.

16

The police station. A map with points marked on to it.
Bryce *pointing to the map and* **Euan** *sitting.*

Bryce   The briefcase was found here, Callum and Maggie's garden.
Here, a man's watch.
Here, here and here, a shirt, a shoe and a soft toy, of Nessie.

Euan   Are they any closer to knowing why it crashed?

Bryce   They'll take months. It's out of my hands now.
I've gathered the information.
But I can't seem to make sense of it myself.

Euan   What was in the briefcase?

Bryce   Maps, a report from the oil company.

Euan   Did you read it?

Bryce   No, it's evidence. I processed it.
I go over it in my mind – watch, shirt, case, toy, shoe.

Because there has to be an answer.
Watch, shirt, case, toy, shoe.

Euan   Where's that report now, Gordie?

Bryce   It's in the safe just now.
With the other evidence.

17

At the Red House.
Jimmy. **Connolly** *has gone, and* **Jimmy** *is waking up amongst his books, after a night of dope smoking and drinking.*
Margaret *enters, looks at him.*

Jimmy   Something of a disappointment in the laird
department.
Aren't I?

Margaret   You could wash.

Jimmy   Does that work?
I'm cold.
We could make a fire.
But I don't know how.

Margaret   I haven't always known privilege, Jimmy.
I wasn't born to it.
But your father saw me by chance in a hotel foyer.
He chose me.
And I assumed it.

Jimmy   Not only you – I've found some of his letters.
He was at it all over the place.

Margaret   He chose me – to be your mother.
There is a difference.

Jimmy   He wasn't interested in convention.
He was moving in directions – thinking in directions
which –

I'm only now beginning to understand – the books – the notes, I've been reading.

Margaret   He had ideas which – were seductive, Jimmy, but they were the products of a disturbed mind.
I was seduced – briefly – as were many people at that time.
But it was a thinking born of despair.
He destroyed himself.
And now you appear to be doing the same.

Jimmy   He was destroyed, because he didn't follow the conventions of privilege. He wouldn't be bound.

Margaret   You don't know what happened.

Jimmy   I will find out.

Margaret   I know what privilege requires because I have been without it.
You don't know, Jimmy.
Because privilege is the air you breathe.
You're unaware of it.
It requires the assumption of authority.
You are part of a line.

Jimmy   I'm the end of the line.

Margaret   Not the end.

Jimmy   The very end.
We have no money left.

Margaret   Money is not what I'm talking about.

Jimmy   We're out of time.
We don't mean anything to anybody any more.

Margaret   I remade this house. I built. I modernised.
This house was at the centre of things.
And I kept it there.
For you to inhabit.
What are you going to do?

Jimmy   I have no choice but to sell.

Margaret   And what about me, Jimmy?

Jimmy   I'm going to take you to Kent.

Margaret   Kent.

Jimmy   Kent's nice. You'll like Kent.

18

Euan *smoking by the tree.*
Norrie *arrives with a briefcase.*

Euan   Did you have any trouble?

Norrie   No trouble.
I waited till Gordie went home.
Climbed in the back window.
I looked around the desk.
I thought – what would Gordie do.
Then I see it.
Photograph of Gordie and his kid.
Code's written on the back.
No problem.
In and out in ten minutes.

Euan   OK. OK. Here.

He gives **Norrie** *some money.*

Two thousand pounds.

He opens the briefcase. Takes papers out. Examines them.

This is good, Norrie, this is movement.
Now.
I need you to do something else for me.

Norrie   What sort of thing?

Euan   Some stalking.

Norrie   Stalking what?

Euan   Connolly.
I want you to shoot him.
Carefully.

Norrie   Shoot him?

Euan   Shoot his hand.

Norrie   Why?

Euan   I've insured Connolly against injury. The guy's my income.
Only I need some ready money now.
I need to move fast on something.
I've seen an opportunity.

Norrie   Connolly's a nice guy. Connolly's . . .

Euan   Connolly's making passes at your wife.

Norrie   How d'you know?

Euan   Spoke to me – asked if he could get Eilish to come to New York with him. Wanted me to fix up the tickets.

Norrie   She never said.

Euan   Course she never said.
Look.
I'm not asking you to kill him.

Norrie   No, to do that, no.
I've taken him into my house.

Euan   Norrie, that is why you can do it.
Shoot his hand, only his right hand.
His left hand's no fucking use to me.
His left hand you don't get paid.
His right hand.

Norrie   It's cold-blooded.

Euan   You cull deer.

Norrie   Aye, but deer. They're deer, like, not fucking folk singers.

Euan   Norrie –
I have a future which is clearly mapped.
And you can be part of that.
This is my offer.

Norrie   I don't know, Euan, this is . . . not for me.

Euan   You've taken a step towards the light, Norrie.
Take the next step.

Norrie   You would do this sort of thing?
It's – I don't believe you would do this.

Euan   You think that way, you keep sinking.
This is making me angry. I don't want to see you sink.
You're a pal.

Norrie   What if I get caught?

Euan   I want you to get caught.
Norrie – you have a motive.
Get yourself drunk. Do it.
And hand yourself in to Gordie.
Any judge in the country understands jealousy.
By the time I've painted Connolly for the skirtchaser he is,
You'll be out with six months max.

Norrie   Two thousand?

Euan   Two thousand and a job as my – right-hand man.
You can be part of this.
Think of you and Eilish, think of what you can do.
Because she wants a man who's capable – Norrie.
And you're losing her. Believe me.

19

Connolly *and* **Eilish** *by the boathouse. Boat hulls upturned. Late afternoon.*

Connolly   I believe we're born and reborn, Eilish.
I believe I've known you, maybe I've . . . connected with you.
Maybe there's no past and no future. Just a circle.

And you and I are walking round each other, Eilish.
Watching each other, all through time.

Eilish   I should be getting back, Norrie'll miss me.

Connolly   You don't want to leave.
You want to be with me.

Eilish   I can't. I have to . . .

Connolly   This, Eilish, is why we've been put here.
This beautiful picture we're in. Boats, the work of man, sea,
the work of nature, but the sea holds the boat like it was a
child.
It's nature. Natural, Eilish.

Eilish   – what I'm feeling – I can't have it.

Connolly   If we don't express our feelings – what are we?
Machines.
Everyone does this.
This is being alive.

Eilish   I want to.
But –

Connolly   I've wanted you the moment I saw you.

Eilish   If it was just once.
One moment of my own.
It wouldn't be wrong. Would it?

Connolly   How could it be wrong?
How could something so natural ever be wrong?

Eilish   One minute that belonged to me.

Connolly   Maybe even two.

After a moment **Eilish** *stands up.*

Connolly   What?

Eilish   Let me look at you.
Make you a picture.
Take it.
Hold it in my head.

20

Bryce *in the police station.*

Bryce   Shoe. Shirt. Toy. Watch. Case.
Toy. Shoe. Shirt. Watch. Case.
Case. Shoe. Watch. Shirt. Toy.
Case. Shoe. Toy. Watch. Shirt.

21

Evening.
Euan *and* **Victoria** *by the tree.*

Euan   Had to get out of the house.
The ticking clock.

He brings out a bottle of wine and opens it.

I didn't bring glasses.
We'll need to take it from the bottle.
This stuff is expensive.
This stuff is the best you can get.

Victoria   No lights.
This must look the same as it's always looked.
Our eyes the first to see it.

Euan   Water – they dream of oil.
And all the time it's the water you wanted.
Deep water you were looking for.
To –
To – happy landings.

Victoria   I've dreamt about you.
These past few days.
My mind's been crazy.

Euan   Of course it has.

Victoria   Dreamt you called me, pulled me out of the sky.

Euan   You came to me, with information.
I acted.

Victoria   You pulled me into that mountainside.
Into that darkness.
Soft ground and water.

Euan   I found you. I took you down the hill.

Victoria   This place – this mountain and sea and forest –
which isn't Illinois. But which – I must have been carrying
with me –
A memory I didn't even have. Maybe you're made of stone.
Rocks have gravity.
Some more than others.
Maybe you're the stone that pulled me in.

Euan   It's meant – I've been thinking about this – it must
be meant.
You being here.
We're given chances.
A moment – and you either take it or you don't.
And we're taking it.

Victoria   In the wreckage. When the world's turning itself
over.
Some people live and some people die.
Some people crawl across the bodies of others.
You would do that.

Euan   I would.

Victoria   I could see that. That's why I recognised you on
the mountain.
You pulled me to you.
Otherwise why was there a mountain there to crash into?
What other reason could there be?

22

The boathouse.
Connolly *sitting smoking.*
Norrie *enters with a shotgun.*

Connolly   Norrie.

Norrie   Shut up. Don't speak.

He points the gun at **Connolly**.

Put your hands up.

Connolly   What the fuck's got into you?

Norrie   Don't speak.
Stand still.

Connolly *stands still, with his hands up.*

Norrie   OK.
OK.
So.
Don't move.
So.

Norrie *can't bring himself to shoot.*

Connolly   Norrie, this is –

Norrie   I SAID DON'T SPEAK.

A moment.
Eilish *emerges from the boathouse.*

Connolly   This is not what . . .

Eilish   Norrie.

Norrie   Fuck.
Fuck.
No.

Eilish   C'mon, we'll go home.
Leave him alone.

We'll go home.
Don't hurt him.

Norrie   I'm taking you to America, Eilish.
America.

A shot, **Connolly**'s *hand is hit.*

23

Oscar *and* **Shona**.

Oscar   My first day in Madrid, Shona.
I saw a tram full of barbers.
Barbers.
Going to the front.
They hadn't even taken off their aprons.
They still had combs in their hands.
I didn't know the barbers had a union even.
Never mind a militia.
And I wondered. Because I really didn't know.
Are they members of the Communist Party?
Or are the barbers anarchists?
But I was so proud to see them.
Proud of myself and proud of human beings.
The tram rattling past me towards the front.
And the barbers inside holding their combs.
On their way to defend the city.
I shouted . . .
'*No Pasaran!*'
At the windows of the tram.
It was only Spanish I knew.
And the barbers beat the tram windows
with the palms of their hands.
They must have soft hands, I thought, being barbers.
I said to myself. In this city everyone's a worker now.
Even barbers are prepared to die for socialism.
To kill for it.
Surely we have to win.

Forty years I held on to that.
Americans come and find oil.
We can't even get ourselves educated.
Can't even own the land.
My son's against me.
I close my eyes and I see myself on the jetty putting a bullet
in that boy.
And still nothing to show for it.

Shona   You've been up at the Red House.

Oscar   Aye.
Thinking.

Shona   Maybe's you shouldn't go there.
If it makes you feel like that.

Oscar   Don't you want it to be ours?

Shona   Want it brought down.
Wish the helicopter had hit it.

Oscar   Still.

Shona   Still.

Oscar   I nearly didn't do it. I nearly didn't. I nearly went
to America.

Shona   It's done. Done.

Oscar   What if I'd taken a different path?
Walked away.
Like that girl.
Stepped out of the wreckage.
Not looked back.

Shona   It isn't what you did, Oscar.
It's what you did it for.

Oscar   I don't remember what I did it for.

Shona   If a thing can't be shifted, best not try to move it.
Best think it's a dream.
Path you're given's the one you've to walk.
All the other paths are dreams.

24

Bright morning.
By the cannon, on the lawn of the Red House.
Jimmy *and* **Euan**.
Jimmy *opens an envelope.*

Jimmy   This is the offer which the council have made me
for the estate.

Euan   I'll add half as much again.

Jimmy   You're very determined.

Euan   It's a simple offer.
What advantage do you have selling to the council?

Jimmy   Some moral advantage.
Bizarrely, my bloodline implies a certain responsibility to
the people of this area.
And your Connolly, he wants a hippie community.
I don't know if I should –

Euan   Connolly is no longer part of the equation, Jimmy.
This is a purchase on my own behalf.

Jimmy   Are you interested in some form of commercial
gain?

Euan   I am interested in developing the loch.

Jimmy   Is that a commercial proposition?

Euan   Very commercial.

Jimmy   Does it confer any advantage to the community?

Euan   Money always does.
Bring money in.
It makes a place work.

Jimmy   I'll accept your offer, Euan.
The highest bidder, everyone had the same chance.
I think that's the fairest way.
One moves with the times.
Not against them.

25

Callum *and* **Maggie** *in their garden looking at the ground.*

Maggie   You'll need to replace that divot.

Callum   It's a big enough divot.

Maggie   Maybe the man from the papers'll want to take a photograph of the dunt.

Callum   I didn't like him too much.

Maggie   Still. Why don't you take a photograph yourself?

Callum   What, just of the ground?

Maggie   Of the hole.

Callum   Just for a record?

Maggie   For us to have a picture.
You said yourself before . . . our future landed on us yesterday.

Callum   It did.

Maggie   We'll have Americans drinking bourbon in our pub.
Rigs in the loch.
Helicopters.

Callum   We'll be like sheiks.

Maggie   Swanning round in Rollses.

Callum   Our little Billy – he'll be an oil man.

Maggie   A lawyer.

Callum   A doctor.

Maggie   A bloody judge
What with this.
It could happen, Callum.

Callum   We should start doing B and B, Maggie.

Maggie   I've always said we should do B and B.

Callum   But now. We could make a feature of the hole. That could be part of the attraction. We could advertise ourselves that way.

Maggie   We're very lucky people, Cal.

Callum   I've always known that.

Maggie   Things just fall into our laps.

Part Three

THE MOUNTAIN

Characters

Victoria, *a wealthy young woman.*
Billy, *a young garage attendant.*
David, *a graduate.*
Maggie, *an unemployed woman. Billy's mother.*
Bryce, *a police constable.*
Kirsty, *a marketing consultant.*
Euan, *the owner of a large quarry.*
Oscar, *an old man.*
Vicky, *David's wife.*
Norrie, *a security guard.*
Patrick, *a security guard.*
Annie, *a protestor.*
Old Victoria
Businessman
Young Euan
Young Oscar

1

Night.
The jetty.
Victoria *emerges from the sea.*
Wearing her underwear, she is wet, cold.

David *offers her his jacket.*
She puts it over herself.

Victoria   I was nearly lost.
Water's icy.

David *offers her a drag of his cigarette, her hands are shaking too much to hold it.*

David *holds it to her lips.*
She drags on it.
She coughs.
She takes a drink of the whisky.

Victoria   Almost didn't come back.
Didn't want to come out.

2

A 747, preparing for take-off.
Old Victoria *and the* **Businessman** *are sitting next to each other.*

The safety instructions are being spoken by a stewardess, in Spanish first then in English.

Old Victoria *is fiddling with the earphones, trying to work out how to plug them in.*

The **Businessman** *attempts to help her.*

Businessman   These plug in here.
Like this.
Now you can tune it to listen to – whatever you want.

Old Victoria   I don't want to listen to anything.
I want to look out of the window.

Businessman   Oh.

Old Victoria   I wanted a window seat.
They gave me this seat.

Businessman   Perhaps there was a mix-up.

Old Victoria   I wanted a window.

Businessman   Perhaps – would you like to swap seats
with me?

Old Victoria   I want to see the water.

They swap seats.
It is a slightly inconvenient procedure.

Businessman   I fly quite regularly.
For work.
My work takes me everywhere.
I don't mind where I sit.
Is this your first time flying?

Old Victoria   Yes.

Businessman   It's really nothing to be concerned about.
It's good you're sitting next to me.
Because if you have any worries.
I'll be able to put your mind at ease.
It's all very routine to me.

Old Victoria   Last time I crossed this water.
I was on a ship.
Moved more slowly.
I just want to see the water.
So I know I'm moving.
The plane takes off.

3

The jetty.
Victoria *and* David *are entwined.*
Victoria *breaks off.*
She drinks from the bottle.

David   You shouldn't drink, you'll lower your body
temperature.
Hypothermia.
And then you'll die.

Victoria   Four years since I've been here.
Since I've sat and watched that sea.

David   Keep warm with me.

Victoria   Used to take my grandad down here.
When he visited.
Never said much.
I always wanted a grandad like in a book.
Where their eyes sparkle and they're wise.
He went blind.
We put him in a home.
Now he's dead.
Thought I'd at least feel – sad or something.

David   What do you feel?

Victoria   Feel cold.

David *puts his arm round her. Holds her.*

Victoria   Don't hold me.

David   I want to hold you.

Victoria   It feels like you're comforting me.
I'm not sad.
I hate funerals when you're not sad.
Shaking hands. Mumbling.

David   I shagged a cousin at a funeral tea once.
The car park of a pub somewhere in Essex.

January.
Black dress.
They had their sandwiches.
I had their daughter.
There's something erotic about funerals.

Victoria   You're sick.

David   You're shivering.
That's what you get for being a sea swimmer.
Fit girl.
Almost healthy.

Victoria   I wanted you to see this place.
Mountains. Sea. Forest.
This is where I grew up.
I wanted you to see me in this place.
What do I look like?

David   Part of the scenery.

Victoria   Do I look like I belong?

David   Like a picture.

He has approached her and again tries to hold on to her.

Victoria   You go away – you come back.
Mountains don't notice.
Might as well never have been there.

4

Morning.
High on the mountain.
Kirsty *and* **Euan** *standing on a cliff above a quarry.*
The rumble of heavy machinery.

Euan   We take granite from the mountain. Mainly we use
explosives. The stone gets processed automatically. The
granite's sent into a machine which crushes the rock into
smaller pieces. The crushing process is repeated until we

have a loose gravel. The gravel's called aggregate. The aggregates are taken down through the mountain, directly beneath our feet, by a conveyor belt. It's taken to a port at the lochside. There it's poured directly into the holds of a container ship. It takes four days to fill a ship. The loads are then shipped out.

Kirsty   Where does the stone go?

Euan   England, to build motorways.
Berlin
New York
Bilbao
All over the world.
This mountain contains three square miles of solid granite.
That's a hundred years supply.
If we only take the far side of the mountain.
Five hundred years if we take the whole mountain.

Kirsty   And you want to take the whole mountain?

Euan   There's plenty mountains here.
I only want one.

Kirsty   The scale, just the scale of the operation takes your breath away.

Euan   The protesters at the gates. They want to stop us expanding.
But if you look down there. What is it they're defending?
A scraping of land on top of rock. There's nothing natural here.
This landscape's been created by sheep and clearance.
Now they say it's beautiful and they want to preserve it.
I think quarrying's beautiful.
We get tourists.
Families stop their cars to watch the granite pouring on to the ships.
I think a line of pylons across a moor is just as elegant as the flight of a bird, or whatever.

Kirsty   If you're profitable, if you have tourists, why do you need me?

Euan   These protesters. They influence the media.
They influence the council.
The application to expand the quarry might be at risk.

Kirsty   But even if you don't expand, you've still got a hundred years supply.

Euan   The profit margin in granite is tiny. It's only stone.
You make your money in the quantities you can sell. A tiny movement in the value of the currency, interest rates, tax, could wipe me out. The larger my operation, the safer I am.

Kirsty   You want me to represent you – to present what – a softer public image?

Euan   This quarry is a simple idea.
To make a living here from farming, or grouse, or whatever – it's like trying to make a living from the moon.
Look around you – sea and rock.
In the seventies I made money from the sea. Used the deep water to build rigs in.
Now I make money from rock.
I use what's there.
Most people aren't able to see the simplicity of this.
They value the barest survival by the most complicated means.
I want them to see the beauty of the obvious.
I want the public to understand that.

Kirsty   Do you believe in it?

Euan   Absolutely.

Kirsty   Then I can help you.

5

A protester's tent by the perimeter fence of the quarry.
Nearby, **Patrick** *and* **Norrie**, *security guards, sit.*

Annie *emerges from the tent, fetches some cold water from a burn.*
Washes herself in it.

Norrie   I've been awake since half past six, Patrick.
I've had my breakfast. I've patrolled the perimeters. I've
completed the crossword and I'm about to take my mid-
morning break with a cup of tea and a Garibaldi.
And those fuckers have only just got up.

Patrick   Maybe that's how they protest.
A sleep-in.

Norrie   It annoys me.

Annie   Morning, Norrie.

Norrie   Don't fucking chat.
Move.

Annie   If you want us to move, Norrie, you'll have to
move us yourself.
Who's the new boy?

Patrick   Hello.
I'm Patrick.

Annie   You just started?

Patrick   Just come up from Glasgow.

Annie   Nice to meet you, Patrick.
Lovely morning.
Mornings like this – you think – it's all worthwile.

Patrick   Aye.

Annie *returns to the tent.*

Norrie   Don't get friendly.

Patrick   Oh right.
Sorry.

Norrie   You'll only have to wade in sometime.
It doesn't help to be friendly.
If you're going to have to hurt them.

Patrick   Are we going to have to hurt them?
They didn't say that at the agency – they said it was basic
security.

Norrie   It is.
Very basic.

6

Morning.
The Red House.
Victoria *and* **Vicky** *with* **Oscar**'s *coffin.*
A Spanish flag draped over it.

Vicky   I think I'd want burned.
Not buried.
Buried would feel like you were waiting for something.
We ought to do it, the way they do in India.
Everybody sees the flames.
We try to hide it.

Victoria   What's the flag mean?

Vicky   A man came from the Spanish Embassy.
They awarded all the international brigades Spanish
citizenship.
Oscar was too ill to go to Spain.
He wanted to go but the doctors wouldn't let him.
After he died. The obituaries and everything.
They came here with all the documents.
They brought the flag.

Victoria   I can't remember what he looks like.
So long since I saw him.

Vicky   That's natural.

Victoria   I close my eyes.
Nothing.
Why are you holding my arm?

Vicky   You'll be feeling – anger.
Sadness.
These are natural stages.

Victoria   What if I'm not, Mum?
What if I'm feeling absolutely nothing at all.
Not even interest.

Vicky   Disbelief is a natural stage.
It'll hit you in time.

Victoria   Didn't know him.
Never talked, not really.
You don't when they're old. Do you?

Vicky   You were away.

Victoria   Did he talk to you?

Vicky   I'm not from here.
He spoke to me.
Never talked.

Billy *enters, wearing his garage uniform, carrying a Co-op bag full of papers.*

Billy   Mrs Sutherland.
Sorry to disturb you.
Hello, Victoria.

Victoria   Billy,
God, Billy.

She hugs him.
He is slightly uncomfortable.

Victoria   I haven't seen you since –
Since . . .

Billy   Few years.

Victoria   I thought you'd gone to Glasgow.
Thought you were – what were you going to do?

Billy   I'm still here.
Working in the garage.

Victoria   We used to drink.
Didn't we –
We used to drink together.
Up the hill with cans of cider.
Mother never knew that.

Vicky   I guessed.

Billy   I'm – sorry about your grandad.

Victoria   Yeah.
Well.
Y'know.

Vicky   Thank you, Billy.

Billy   I brought this.
It's – it was Oscar's.
Don't really know what to do with it.
Thought I'd better give it to you.

He gives her the Co-op bag.

Victoria   An inheritance?

Vicky   He didn't have any money.

Victoria   Don't look at me like that.
I was being ironic.
What is it?

Billy   It's just some stuff he wrote.
He used to tell me stories down the pub.
I was interested so he asked me to write them down for him.
He said he wanted to make it into a book.
I thought I'd better give it to you.
It's not mine to keep.
His words.

Victoria   I didn't know you knew him?

Billy   Not really.
Just wrote stuff down for him.

Vicky   It's good of you to come by, Billy.
Stay –

Billy   S'all right.
I'm . . . sorry.

Vicky   Stay – why don't you eat with us – we're going up
to the hotel for lunch.

Billy   I'd better get back to work.
Thanks.
Well – see you.

Victoria   We'll go for a drink?

Billy   If you want.

Victoria   I do.

Billy   You know where I am.

Billy *leaves.*

Vicky   Such a strange boy.
So little energy.
All this work.

Victoria *takes the papers out of the bag.*
Opens a notebook.

Oscar   My first day in Madrid.
I'd never seen sunshine like it.
Blue sky –

Victoria *shuts the book.*

Vicky   He's still here, Victoria.
They stay.
They stay with us.
I'll leave you with him.
You can talk to him in private.

Say what you need to say.

Vicky *leaves.*
Victoria *looks at the coffin.*
Doesn't say anything.

7

The perimiter fence.
Patrick *is trying to drag* **Annie** *away.*
Her body is stiff.
Resistant.
Patrick *stops.*
He puts **Annie** *down.*

Patrick   Stay there.
I need a fag.

He reaches into his jacket to get a fag. He lights up.

Want one yourself?

Annie   Cheers.

Patrick   You only get it if you promise not to run back to
the fence.

He gives her a cigarette.

Where's it you're from, Annie?

Annie   Nottingham.

Patrick   Never been. Nice place?

Annie   I haven't been back since I left school.
I lived in London for a bit.
Then I did this.
Been moving ever since.

Patrick   D'you see your folks ever?

Annie   Never.

Patrick   Here – d'you want a brew?
I'll get one.

Patrick *gets a thermos of tea. Pours two cups.*

Annie   Always tastes better from a flask.
Perfect on a day like this.

Patrick   You know – I've only to get you over there.
You could walk.
Save us both fighting.

Annie   I can't do that.

Patrick   Suppose.
And I have to move you.
We do what we do.

Annie   You don't have to work for them.

Patrick   First job I've had, Annie – first job for years.
Things are a bit fucked up for me back home.
I saw the agency, chance to live somewhere else.
Get a bit of money.
You've got to take what you can get.

Annie   Think about what you're defending, Patrick.
The hill's been here for millions of years.
Longer than humans.
Sutherland wants to take it all for himself.

Patrick   Mountain doesn't mean that much to me.
Hard to walk up it.
Hard to walk down.
It's a workplace.
If you win – I'm on the next bus home.
Simple as that.

Annie   We're trying to protect it for you as well, for
everyone.
For the future.

Patrick   Don't get me wrong. That's OK. You believe
in it.

That's fair enough. Maybes I'm wrong anyway.
Do you want a biscuit?

Annie   How come you're nice to us, and Norrie's such a
bastard?

Patrick   Ach, Norrie's OK.
He just takes it too seriously.
His wife ran off to America while he was in prison for GBH
or something.

Annie   GBH. Jesus.

Patrick   He's not like that but.
He's not really a GBH kinda guy, if you ask me.
He gets pissed every night in the Portakabin watching yous
all having a laugh.
He wakes up with a hangover and he sees yous all sleeping
yours off.
It just annoys him.
I'm trying to get him on to dope.
Calm him down.

Annie   Very public-spirited of you.

Patrick   OK. I suppose we'd better get on with it.

Annie   I'm ready if you are.

Patrick   Right, I'm taking you over there, beyond the
perimeter.

Annie *allows him to grab her under the arms.*
He struggles with her.
Drags her off.

8

Lunch.
Victoria, **David Vicky** *and* **Euan**.
Eating in a restaurant.

Euan   So, David, you write – ?

David   Yes.

Euan   And what do you actually do?

David   Freelance work.
Travel. Criticism. Interviews.

Victoria   He's writing a book.

David   I'm thinking about it but . . .

Vicky   A book – what about?

David   It's more of a long-term plan.

Victoria   His idea is a history of the twentieth century,
told from the point of view of a man's jacket.

David   This was one idea.

Victoria   The jacket moves from person to person.

David   It's a device.

Vicky   I think that's an amazing idea. I think that's
beautiful.
Have you – experienced that idea?

David   I – thought it up.

Euan   This is what you're working at?

David   Journalism is the main thing.

Euan   You earn a living?

David   I try.

Euan   You have to keep moving.

Vicky   I admire your energy, David.

David   Thank you.

Euan   This writing – this is something I investigated in the
past.

It's a field I know something about. Not the writing. But the entertainment industry. The key is to move ahead of the market. To see what's coming – to see simple ideas which – are ahead of their time.

David   I completely agree with that.

Victoria   That's what David does. He does that.

Euan   What about you?

Victoria   Me?

Euan   Have you decided what you want to do?

Victoria   I'm trying.

Euan   Why are you telling me you're trying?
I see no direction, I see stabbing movements, back and forth. Try this, try that . . . this word 'try' comes back to me. I don't like it. Try is attempt. Attempt says to me 'failure'.

Victoria   I haven't found anything worth doing yet.

Euan   I see no – forward movement in your life.

Victoria   Forward to what?

Euan   You've been to university. I paid for this.
Now you've changed your mind?
You've given up.
What were you doing?

Vicky   Psychology.

Euan   You going to be a psychologist?

Victoria   You don't study psychology to be a psychologist.

Euan   What then.

Victoria   You study it to – understand people.

Euan   All you need to understand people,
is to understand this.

Euan *takes out his wallet.*
Takes out money.
Puts it on the table.

Euan   You have too much money.
No hunger.
Full stomach.
That's psychology.

9

On the 747.
Old Victoria *and the* **Businessman**.

Businessman   I hope you don't mind me asking.
Your accent.
Are you Scottish?

Victoria   I am.

Businessman   Keith Cooper.
Glasgow.
I work in construction.
What's your name?

Victoria   Victoria.

Businessman   Victoria.
Which part of Scotland do you hail from, Victoria?

Victoria   The Highlands.
A small place.
You wouldn't know it.

Businessman   Lovely part of the world up there.
My wife and I have a holiday cottage near Oban.
I think of it as home.
I do.
The mountains, the sea, the forest.

He takes a photograph out of his wallet.

This is it.
My wife – my sons.
We're just about to go walking.
Of course the place is overrun with people from
Manchester, nowadays.
We'll probably retire up there.

Victoria   Manchester?
People from Manchester?

Businessman   Nice people – but they don't . . .
understand.
Were you on holiday in Argentina, Victoria?

Victoria   Holiday.
Yes. I was.

Businessman   I've been working.
Good to be going back.
I'm going for the football.
Scotland are playing – few of the colleagues.
Bit of a hooly.
I don't suppose you follow the football?

Victoria   I went to a match in 1978.
My son took me.
It was terribly dispiriting.

Businessman   The joy of leaving is the coming home.
Train crosses the Clyde, pulls in to Central.
– the cranes – the bridges –
Never fails to move me.

Victoria   Every mile of sea, I've been watching it,
I can feel the weight of it.

Businessman   Always like that at the end of a holiday.
Back to the real world.

Victoria   The same sea I looked at.
Same one.

10

The funeral.
Mourners around the graveside.
At a slight distance, **Billy** *smoking.*
Victoria *leaves the group and approaches him.*

Victoria   Got a fag?

Billy *gives her a cigarette.*

Billy   It isn't right – the service – it isn't what he wanted.

Victoria   I can't stand it.
Listening to myself singing hymns, I don't know.
Putting a face on.

Billy   He didn't want religion.
Oscar.
He told me.
He said he wanted no ministers.
– he said –

Victoria   You talked to him about it?

Billy   Yeah.

Victoria   How come he talked to you, Billy?
All my life – his torn face –
How come he talked to you?

Billy   I liked him.

Victoria   You look good, Billy.
Black suit.
Better than that numpty outfit from the garage.

Billy   You look good.

Victoria   I can't believe you're still here.
You stayed all this time?

Billy   Yeah.

Victoria   Did you miss me?

Billy　You go away, Vic, people carry on.
We don't just stop.
. . .
Who's your boyfriend?

Victoria　David.
He's from college.
He's OK.
. . .
When you talked to Oscar.
And he said he didn't want religion.
What did he say he wanted?

Billy　Said he wanted his ashes in Spain.
And he said no ministers – no hymns –
You should read what he wrote.
No eulogies.
Just an expression of hope.

Victoria　He's dead.
So he doesn't care.

Billy　I care.

Victoria　It's a small thing.

Billy　Big or small.
Depends where you stand, doesn't it?
Something he wanted your father didn't.
When he stopped building the rigs.
And my dad was struggling for the rent.
He stopped the tenancy.
From our house you can see the mountain.
My mother likes the view.
It's a small thing.
But your father wants it quarried.
You people always win.

Victoria　You're angry with me?

Billy　Never said that.
. . .

You staying long, Vic?

Victoria   Maybe. You want me to?

Billy   Just curious.
Heard you'd dropped out.

Victoria   Didn't see the point.

Billy   What you going to do?

Victoria   Try and find something worth doing.

The mourners have started moving away from the grave.

You coming to the tea at the hotel?

Billy   Aye. S'pose.

Victoria   Meet me in the car park.
While they're having their sandwiches.
We'll have a smoke or something.
Will you come?

Billy   Might do.

*As the mourners leave, some of them shake **Victoria***'s hand.*
They mumble.
She mumbles.
The crowd clears.
She stays.
Euan *is at the grave.*
Oscar *is sitting on it.*

Euan   Vicky thinks this place is haunted.
Thinks there's memory in the stones.
Thinks she sees fucking events, historical events.
I own this place.
I own the fucking sea and the fucking mountain and the
forest.
This place is mine.
So don't . . . don't . . . come back.
I own these fucking historical events which take place in
Vicky's fucking head in this fucking place.

So don't come back.
Close my eyes and I don't want to see you.
Close my eyes and you'll be gone.

Oscar *doesn't move.*

11

The hotel car park.

Billy, **David** *and* **Victoria** *sharing a joint.*

Victoria   Imagine there's been a fire.
Fire's taken everything with it.
Everything human.
A fire that kills only humans – and it's us left.
The two of us alone, here.
The mountains, the sea, the forest.
How long would we survive?

Billy   Not long, Vic, not me. Not without fags.

Victoria   We could make fags. Grow leaves. Dry them in
the sun.

David   Is tinned food destroyed in this fire?
I mean, if we could raid supermarkets.
We'd have everything.

Victoria   What if enemies came – bands of survivors?
What if they wanted to attack us?
There's nobody, nobody to protect us.

Billy   I'd run. Hide. Surrender.

David   We're intelligent. We could use our intelligence to
make weapons. The secret would be to advance our
technology as fast as possible.

Billy   What – throw tins at their heads.

Victoria   Who'd fight? Would you fight?

Billy Maybes they wouldn't be hostile, these other people.
Maybes they'd be . . . all right.

David We could construct defences – do libraries exist?
Do books survive this fire?

Victoria I'd fight.

Billy What for?
If there's nobody left.
Nothing to fight for.

David Can I take a computer?

Victoria Why?

David To write, that'd be my luxury.

Victoria Why?

David Because I'd want to.

Victoria Why?

David To record everything, to create.

Victoria Why?

David To pass the time.

Victoria Just the three of us. I was thinking it.
Car park gone.
Hotel gone.
No lights. No houses.
Just the mountains, the sea and the forest.
Everyone else dead. Everything gone. That's what I want.

Billy Just as long as there's booze, Vic.

12

The lawn of the Red House.
Vicky *and* **Kirsty** *drinking herbal tea.*

Vicky   He took me back through my childhood.

Kirsty   Right. God.

Vicky   I regressed.
You have to imagine it like a video of your life set on
rewind.

Kirsty   Right. Ugly.
I mean, it would be for me.
What a sight.

Vicky   So he took me back and back, even into the womb.

Kirsty   You remembered the womb?

Vicky   Even to the sperm and the egg and then . . .
Back into my past lives.

Kirsty   I can barely remember past yesterday.
I need hypnosis to remember where I put my purse.

Vicky   I felt sun on my face.
And a hot wind.
I opened my eyes and I saw desert and in the distance a train
of camels, and men, and brightly coloured flags. A caravan.
I felt a pain.
I looked down on my feet and saw jewelled slippers.
And then I remembered.
I was the concubine of a wealthy trader.
He sold spices between Persia and Jerusalem.
I was walking through the desert.

Kirsty   How awful.

Vicky   That's where my pain had come from.
The walking.
The endless walking in the desert.

Kirsty   This was all in your head?

Vicky   The most amazing part of it was . . .
Recently I'd been reading about the holy land.
The secrets of the desert and the ancient gods.
And I didn't know why I was drawn to these images.
I didn't know.
But there it was staring me in the face.
I had belonged to the desert in a past life.

Kirsty   It's amazing to think you could remember.

Vicky   The word remember comes from Latin.
Remember. So remembering is like another way of saying
putting your body back together.

Kirsty   God.

Vicky   Our bodies hold memories, the same way the earth
holds fossils. In the quarry, you can find fossils in the rock.
The shapes of creatures from before time.
It's the same with our us, past lives are laid down amongst
the blood almost.
Think about your body.

Kirsty   Awful.

Vicky   Think. Close your eyes. Shh.

They are quiet for some moments.

Keep your eyes closed.
Which part of your body do you feel?

Kirsty   I don't know . . .

Vicky   Think about being five years old.

Kirsty   I am.

Vicky   Is part of you . . . tingling. Like pins and needles.
You have to concentrate.

Kirsty   My calf.
Oh God, my calf's tingling.
What does that mean?

Vicky   I'm not trained but . . .
It means your body holds its memories of childhood in your
calf area. That's common for childhood. The leg area
generally is common.

Kirsty   I'm not too weird then?

Vicky   Not weird at all.
When I was taken back to the womb. I hold the womb in
my solar plexus region. I was told to massage myself there to
stimulate the memories. You could massage your leg, for
instance.

Kirsty   It's so . . . just . . .
I wish I had more time to be involved in these cults.
I love my car.
That's my cult.

Vicky   Regression isn't a cult. It's a therapy.

Kirsty   Yes.
My car's my therapy.
It's the only place I have time to think.
On motorways I enter a Zen place, you know, a place of
meditation.

Vicky   You have to be careful on the road.

Kirsty   Oh, of course I don't actually meditate while I'm
driving.

Vicky   These techniques touch very emotional parts of
you.
They unbury things.
You can become very distressed.

Kirsty   Does everyone have buried things?

Vicky   Oh yes.

Kirsty   I get migraines sometimes.

Vicky   The head is the locus of your pain.
Your mind carries hurt.

That's very typical.
If you unbury that hurt. The migraines will go away.

Kirsty   You know, I think I'll look into that.
You must give me the name of this Edinburgh woman you
see.
Migraines don't help me in my work.

Vicky   You're very open. That's a good start.
For the healing to work you have to be open all the time.

Kirsty   Like an all-night garage?

Vicky   Yes. Yes just like an all-night garage.

13

After the funeral.
Maggie*'s kitchen table.*
A small telly on in the corner, sound turned down.
Billy *has changed into his workwear, red trousers, a white shirt, a red
bow tie and a red cap.*
A small pile of money in front of **Maggie**.

Billy   Have you counted the gas?

Maggie   That's everything.

Billy *puts the money into a jar.*

Billy   I'll keep it. Take it into the bank later and pay it over.

Maggie   Car's got no petrol in it, Billy.

Billy   We've no money for petrol.
We need what's left for food.

Maggie   And drink.
There's some for drink, isn't there?

Billy   Course, Mum.

Maggie   But not for petrol.

Billy   No.

Maggie   When you going to get rich, Billy?
I need you to get rich so's you can look after me.

Billy   You just have to stop driving around, Mum.
We can't afford it.

Maggie   I like it.

Billy   Joyriding.
It's s'posed to me that bloody joyrides.
Not you.
I'm s'posed to steal them and set them on fire.
I need to go to work.

Maggie   You shouldn't be working.
You should be at college.
Your dad thought you'd the brains to be a lawyer.
You should just go – leave me here – I'd be all right.

Billy   Give me the car keys.

Maggie   Car's got no petrol. I told you.

Billy   Gary'll never notice if I take some from the garage.
S'there enough to get me to the garage?

Maggie   I think so.

Billy   You got fags?

Maggie   No.

Billy   Here.

He gives her five cigarettes from his packet.

Maggie   You be back tonight?

Billy   Might be late.

Maggie   You seeing Victoria.

Billy   Might.

Maggie   You were good with her.
A handsome couple.

Billy   I'm not sleeping with her.

Maggie   Don't sleep, Billy.
Stay awake.
She's quick.
She's rich.
You can catch her.
Keep your eyes open.

Billy   I'd better go else I'll be late.

14

Victoria *and* **David** *on a boat, in the loch.*
Victoria *reading from* **Oscar***'s papers.*
Oscar *is present in the scene. Sitting.*

David   This is a gold mine.
I didn't believe you when you said he'd fought in Spain.
But to see this material.

Oscar   Most days that spring we spent in the trench. Euan
was commissar of our unit and he'd arranged for us to have
some of the better accommodation on the lines but when
the rain came in March our clothes were perpetually soaked
through and we spent many nights cold to the bone. The
fascist artillery was landing close to the lines but we were
sending our own artillery out and a flow of deserters came
across to us from their lines. Sometimes they brought
American cigarettes with them –

Victoria *shuts the book.*

Victoria   You interested?

David   You never asked him about this?
It's unbelievable.

Victoria   You a communist?

David   I sort of am.

I've always had a soft spot for, you know, Orwell, Spender,
these people.
This could be published. The story here . . .

Victoria   What is it?

David   What?

Victoria   Communism?

David   I'm more of a Marxist – if anything.

Victoria   I mean, I know what it looks like.
It's like Prague or something.
But what is it?
Reading this – I can't get it to mean anything.

David   I thought you did this in foundation year.

Victoria   Must be thick.
Not like you.

David   Read some more.

She chooses a page at random.

Oscar   The villagers brought out the committee of six
men who'd been running the village. There was some
debate amongst the comrades and the villagers before it was
agreed that they were to be executed. A volunteer detail,
myself included, was sent to complete the job. Some of the
men complained at doing this work but we were all aware
that there was a wider aim and that each step along the
road was a step towards achieving it for all of us. We
executed the men at dawn.

She shuts the book.

David   This is incredible. Are you going to use this
stuff?
You could – I could – write this up.
I'd love to have a proper look at it.

Victoria   You want it?

David   It could be worth something.

Victoria   I don't need money.

David   Vic, I was thinking.
When we go back.
I've got to go back to London, day after tomorrow.
I've got an interview lined up with Channel Four.
I don't really want to take the job but –
–
I thought you could come back with me.
We could move in together.

Victoria   I thought you wanted to write.

David   I do but –
I'm broke just now.
But with your money – we could . . .
Buy a place.
I could pay you rent or something.

He takes her silence for an answer.
David *starts to row.*

Victoria   Your skinny body.
I love your skinny body.

David   Let's go back in to shore.

Victoria   Let's not.

David   It's getting late.

Victoria   Take your clothes off.

David   It's a bit cold, Vic.

Victoria   Do as you're told.

David   Let's go inside.

Victoria   No – let's do this – I want to try this.
On a boat.

David   Are you going to take your clothes off as well?

Victoria   I know you too well.
You're a dog.
How much do you want?

David   What?

Victoria   How much money.
To take your clothes off for me.

David   More than you've got.
It's too cold.

Victoria *takes out her cheque book.*

Victoria   How about a hundred?

David   How about two?

Victoria   OK.

David   You're joking.

Victoria *writes the cheque. Gives it to him.*

David   I don't want your money.

Victoria   You don't need to do a job, David.
I won't let you.
I'll pay for you.
I'll be a writer's moll –
I'll be your inspiration.
Take it.

David   I wasn't asking to be looked after.
I was asking you to move in with me.
In the normal way.

Victoria   I'm not normal.

She holds the cheque over the edge of the boat.
He takes it from her.

David   You're bad.

Victoria   Bad.
Yes.

We'll go inside.
To my room.
We'll go there now.
I want to row.
Give me the oars.

She starts to row.

15

Euan *and* **Kirsty** *in an office.*
Looking at a computer screen.

Kirsty   These pictures don't look like you, Euan.
They look like publicity shots.

Euan   They are publicity shots.

Kirsty   That's not good.
You look good as you are.
You should dress as you are.
We'll get some new shots done.
Some with your family, with your wife.
Your daughter.

Euan   Not my wife.

Kirsty   OK, if you want to protect her.

Euan   I want to protect me.
She's insane.
Past lives – all that –
Don't want the press getting hold of that.

Kirsty   Rock is a hard image, explosives are destructive.
The image is warfare against nature.
You project hardness in these pictures.
You're defensive.
In these interviews you're cold, you hold back.
Rock.
That's not the way you talk to me.

Euan   They ask such stupid questions –

Kirsty   People suspect you're hiding something when they see these photographs. When they read this press.

Euan   I am hiding things.

Kirsty   You have to be honest, Euan.

Euan   I thought this was public relations.

Kirsty   I know, we have a reputation.
That reputation is old-fashioned. That's in the past.
Now, PR is about truth.
People are tired of lies. They can see through distortion.
Ninety per cent of my job now is persuading clients to be honest with people.
Do you have anything to hide, Euan?

Euan   No.

Kirsty   Are you ashamed of anything?

Euan   No.

Kirsty   Then why should anyone want to stop you?

Euan   It's the same old fight – people like me, who create money, and people like them, who want to take it from me.

Kirsty   Euan – those words are attack – we don't attack. We help.
Our job is to help the council to find the right answer to this problem. Which we will do.
Because our answer is correct.

16

Victoria *and* **David** *in bed.*
Victoria *with* **Oscar**'s *book.*
David *asleep.*
Oscar *sitting separate.*

The sound of a battle. Gunfire. Artillery. Aeroplane overhead.

Young Oscar *and* **Young Euan** *enter, crawling along the ground carrying rifles.*

Young Euan   There.

Young Oscar   Where?

Young Euan   Down there.
In the corrie.

Young Oscar   I see them.

Young Euan   They don't see us yet.

Young Oscar   They will as soon as we shoot.

Young Euan   They'll move that way – towards the burn.
After the first shot –
Aim there.
Are you ready?

Young Oscar   Aye.

Young Euan *and* **Young Oscar** *both shoot. They fire again.*
A hail of gunfire at them.
They scramble for cover.

Young Euan   Shit, shit. Run.

Young Oscar   I can't.

Young Euan   Run, fuck's sake.

Young Oscar   I can't.
I can't move.

Young Euan   Are you hit?

Young Oscar   I've shit myself.

Young Euan   Oh Christ.
Just move.

Young Oscar   I don't want to.

Young Euan   Do it.

Young Oscar   I don't want to.

Young Euan   They've seen us.
You've got to move.

Young Oscar   I DON'T WANT TO.

Young Euan *stands up, trying to pull* **Young Oscar** *to his feet.*
Young Euan *is shot.*
He falls.

Young Euan   Oh Christ.
Christ.

Young Oscar *moves over to him. Holds on to him.*

Young Euan   Will you run, Oscar, for fuck's sake.

Old Oscar *who has been watching the scene, speaks.*

Old Oscar   I couldn't move any more.
I stayed where I was.
Not through courage.
But through fear.
I didn't want to be alone.
They must have thought we were both dead because they
stopped firing at us.
I stayed till nightfall.
When it was dark, I tried to carry Euan back to the lines.

Young Oscar *lifts up* **Young Euan**, *tries to carry him.*

Young Oscar   We're losing this.

Young Euan   No, we're not.

Oscar   They tore through us. We're losing.

Young Euan   My first day in Madrid, Oscar.
I saw a tram full of barbers.
Barbers.
Going to the front.
They hadn't even taken off their aprons.
They still had combs in their hands.
I didn't know the barbers had a union even.

Never mind a militia.
And I wondered. Because I really didn't know.
Are they members of the Communist Party.
Or are they anarchists?
But I was proud to see them.
Proud of myself and proud of us.
The tram.
And the barbers.
On their way to defend the city.
Oscar,
Even the barbers are prepared to fight for socialism.
We have to win.

17

Maggie *by the side of a road.*
Radio hiss.
Constable Bryce *shines a torch in her face.*

Bryce   Maggie.

Maggie   Callum, is that you?

Bryce   No, it's me – Gordie Bryce.

Maggie   Gordie.

Bryce   You run out of petrol again?
S'the gauge broken?

Maggie   Must be.
Only wanted to get as far as the lighthouse.

Bryce   I'll give you lift home.
C'mon.
Billy can come out and pick up the car in the morning.

18

In an Esso garage.
Billy *working behind the counter.*
Victoria *comes in, smoking.*

Billy   You can't smoke, Vic.

Victoria   . . .

Billy   It's my job to say. I have to.
. . .
D'you want a packet of crisps or something?
A can?

Victoria   No.

Billy   You sure?

Victoria   All right.

Billy   Wait then. Just look like you're browsing.
Wait till the camera's going the other way.

Victoria   Take a fucking look at these crisps.
People put this stuff inside them.
What's the relationship between this and a potato?
This thing hasn't even met a potato.

Billy   All right.

He nips out from behind the counter. He takes a packet of crisps and a can of drink. He gives them to **Victoria**. *Just as the camera swings back he pretends to put money in the till.*

Victoria   You could lose your job, nicking.
I've got the money anyway. I could've paid.

Billy   I like stealing from them.

Victoria   What would a crisp look like if it was pure?
What would it taste like?

Billy   I don't know, Vic.

Victoria   D'you get wild potatoes?

Billy   There must have been at one time.

Victoria   You could slice up a wild potato.
And fry it in . . .
Some fat from a wild animal.
Like a fox.
Fry it on a flat stone.
Heated in a wood fire.

Billy   Still, a crisp, Vic. It's just a crisp.

Victoria   They collapse evenly in your mouth.
Each one mushes up the same way.
I can't eat any more of these.
There must be somewhere you can go –
Somewhere there isn't crisps.

Billy   Maybes Africa.

Victoria   I've been to Africa.
There was crisps.

Billy   I'd like to go, one day.

Victoria   Come – come with me.
I'll take you.
We'll go now.

Billy   I'm working.

Victoria   Leave the job.

Billy   I need the money.

Victoria   I've got money.

Billy   I can't take your money.
Anyway, I need to look after my mum.

Victoria   I hate seeing you working here.
It isn't fair.
What d'you want?
I'll give it you. A loan even. Whatever.

Billy   I can't. Vic. I'm sorry.

Victoria   Bow tie.
You don't need a bow tie to do your job.
Why d'you wear that?

Billy   I have to.

Victoria   Have to?
Nobody should have to do anything.
That's what I believe. What's that? To believe that?
Is it communist?

Billy   No, it's not communist.

Victoria   What is it then?

Billy   It's childish, Vic.

Victoria   That's what I'll be then.
Even if it's only me.
Childish.
Party of one.

Victoria *leaves*.

19

Morning.
Norrie *and* **Patrick** *in a Portakabin*.
Patrick *is smoking a joint*.
Norrie *is drinking whisky*.

Patrick   You want some, Norrie?

Norrie   No.

Patrick   Listen.
That's my shift started.
You've no need to stay, Norrie –
If you want to get to the pub.
Watch the football.

Norrie   I'll just finish this.

Annie *enters*.

Annie   Norrie.

Patrick   Norrie was just – finishing his drink.

Norrie   Very cosy.

Annie   I'll go.

Norrie   Very fucking cosy.

Patrick   We're just having a smoke.
It's cool.
I'll move her on tomorrow.

Norrie   The pair of you.
You're protecting a hill.
A fuckin slab of stone.
I tell you – I live here.
Live here, born here and fucking wasted away here.
That hill.
Happy if it's blown up tomorrow.
Happy if the whole place is put on one of those ships and
sunk.
And you – you're protecting the property of Mr Euan
Sutherland.
Who is the greatest cunt upon this earth.
And now the pair of you are going to fuck each other.
Well, you both deserve it.
You both deserve to get fucked.

Norrie *gets his coat and goes to leave.*

Annie   You going to tell on Patrick, Norrie?

Norrie   Who to?

Annie   Sutherland.

Norrie   Fuck him.
Fuck the lot of yous.
I'm resigning.
I know where I belong.

I belong with the wasters.

Norrie *exits with his bottle.*
Patrick *looks out after him.*

Annie   I should have been watching to see if he'd gone.

Patrick   He's going over to the tents.
He's sat down with the boys.
He's handing out the whisky.
Fucker's become a hippie.
You've turned him hippie.
You've turned him.

20

A meeting room in the council offices.
Kirsty *in front of a committe of local councillors.*

Kirsty   I'm sure you understand, given the recent tragic
death of his father, who was a colleague of yours at one
time, that Mr Sutherland can't be with us today. So I'm
here to speak on behalf of Sutherland Granite Aggregates.
In our previous evidence you have heard about the necessity
for a second quarry, the economic benefits to the local area
and the employment opportunities. We've also told you
about our plans to minimise the environmental impact of
such a development. I don't intend to go over that ground
again. What I am here to say is that we have considered the
objections of the environmental lobby and we have taken
some of their worries on board. It is as a direct response to
these worries that we have included a new element to our
proposal. The Oscar Sutherland Business Training Centre.
I refer you to Diagram One of the presentation. Mr
Sutherland has decided that if the proposal for a second
quarry goes ahead, then he will build for the community a
training centre, fully staffed, and will give out grants of five
thousand pounds to young local people with business ideas
that can be located in the West Highlands. I refer you to

Diagram Two. The funding for this centre will come from
the profits from the second quarry, if it goes ahead. Mr
Sutherland feels such an initiative will do justice to the
memory of his father, whose life was dedicated to increasing
opportunity for all, and to the community in which he
himself was brought up. I therefore submit our application
for your consideration.

21

The pub.
Evening.
A television on showing international football.
It is the beginning of the match.
The camera is following the team as it sings the anthem.
Flower of Scotland

Euan *is watching.*
Maggie *is watching.*
Norrie *is watching.*
Patrick *is watching.*
Bryce *is watching.*
David *and* **Billy** *are watching.*

By the tree, sitting on a stone, with the Co-op bag, smoking,
Victoria.

Old Oscar *sits near her.*

Victoria   Winning and losing.
Small things.
It just depends on where you stand.
One step across that water.
I could leave you.
In the same earth you're made of.
Like a stone in the ground.
Step across the water.
But you'd follow me.
Stone in my head.

Not talking.
Weight of your life.
Weight of this place.
There was a fire and you fought.
Granada, Madrid, Huesca, Barcelona.
I'm your defeat.

Oscar *sits, holds her.*

Victoria   Stone too heavy to carry.
Can't go forward.
Me and all that made me.
The weight of oldness.
This place.
If I could step out of my body.
Leave my skin and bone on the hillside.
Walk into some new life.
But I'm half in and half out of the ground.
Place holds me.
The shape of me.
In the mountainside.

She breaks away from him.

I'll not carry you.
Stone in my head. Cold.
I'll not carry you.

In the pub.
The match is finished.
A groan of dissapointment.

Kirsty *enters, goes straight to* **Euan**.

Euan   We always lose.
I hate that.
There's nothing admirable in losing.
They love it.
It turns my stomach.

Kirsty   We won.
You got the permission.
They've bought the idea.

Euan   You sure?

Kirsty   Sure.

He kisses her.
He moves.

Euan   Norrie! Norrie get here.

22

Night.
The cemetery.
Victoria, **David** *and* **Billy**.
Billy *with a spade.* **Victoria** *with a spade.*
David *without.*

David   There are procedures – we can – I've heard about this.
You can register . . .

Victoria   Dig.

David   I'm just saying . . .

She gives him a spade.
Billy *begins to dig.* **David** *does, half-heartedly.*

David   The man is dead. He is gone. He has no wishes.
And this . . . this is extreme. What you're asking us to do here, Vic. This goes beyond – because you're feeling grief – that's understandable.

Billy   I need to be pissed to do this.

Billy *takes a swig from a bottle of whisky.*

David   This is primitive. This is . . . I can't do this.
You do it.
If you want to do it.

Victoria   I know I can do it.
I want to know if you can do it.

David   No.
No.
This is – both of you – have taken this to a point – I have
respect – I came here to show respect for a person,
admiration even, but – this is too – real, this is robbing a
grave.

Billy   S'what Oscar wanted.

David   I can't do it.

Victoria   You'd better go then.

David *hesitates*.

David   What is there in this place? Jesus. Never been in a
place so fucking dark before.
The whole place is fucking darkness and bog.

Victoria   I want you to go.

David   Don't know which way.

Billy   Follow the road.
Till you see lights.
Head for the lights.

David   If I go, I'm going, Victoria.
I'm not . . .
. . .

Billy   Just go.

David   You're too – she is – pushing too far.

David *goes*.

Billy   Need to be very pissed.

He takes another swig.
The sound of wood tearing.
Victoria *gets into the grave*.

Victoria   Remember what he looks like now.

They look at **Oscar***'s body.*

Billy *lights a fag.*

Victoria   We'll take him up the mountain.
I know a place.
Burn him there.

23

The tent.
Norrie *beside the tent.*
With a torch.
And a can of petrol.

Norrie   You'd better come out.

Annie *comes out of the tent.*

Norrie   We're to burn the camp.
Sutherland's orders.

Annie   We lost the appeal.

Norrie   What're you going to do?
Go somewhere else?

Annie   We're staying.

Norrie   What's the point if you've lost the appeal.

Annie   We make trouble. We continue to make trouble.
That's the way we work. We don't let it be easy.

Norrie   That's what I thought.
Annie, I have keys.
I can let you into the site.
Summer night.
A fire can spread, you know.

Annie   Spread where?

Norrie   I'll show you.

Norrie *points to a control room behind the fence.*
The rumble of machinery.

Norrie   That's where it's controlled from.
The machinery's on.
It runs through the night.

Annie   What do I do?

Norrie   Go inside. Pour the petrol around.
Then come out.
Don't smoke.
This is your chance.

Annie   He'll only repair it.

Norrie   He'll repair it tomorrow.
Tonight he'll be cursing.

Annie *exits*.

24

Victoria *and* **Billy** *carrying* **Oscar**'s *body*.
Billy *carrying a can of petrol*.

Victoria   Imagine the sea, Billy.
Imagine coming in off the sea in a boat made of wood.
Coming up to the beach.
To a house that you'ld built.
Imagine we were the only people left.
Place without a name left even.
Nothing was touched or spoiled.
Nothing to eat that wasn't caught or grown by us.
Nothing to read that wasn't written by us.
Nothing but us.

Billy   I like people, Vic.
I like most people.

Victoria   With me.
Only us.
Everyone else dead.

They lay **Oscar**'s *body on the ground*.

Victoria Here.

Billy Thank fuck. I'm knackered.
I'm pissed.
What're we going to do now, Vic?
Going to burn him now?

Victoria Burn him,
Gather the ashes and take them to Spain.
To the places he said in his book.

Victoria *pours petrol over* **Oscar**'s *body.*
Billy *gives her his bottle.*
She takes a swig.
She takes out a cigarette.
She lights it.

Billy You want to be alone?
You want me to be here?

Victoria I want you to be here.

Billy *sits.*

Victoria See the night, Billy, and the mountain and it's
still warm.
Like it used to be when we came up here with cider.
Do you still like me?

Billy Yes.

Victoria Do you want me?

Billy Yes.

Victoria Will you sleep with me?

Billy Christ, Vic, but . . .

Victoria I know you do.
Always have.
Billy, take this.
I brought this for you.

She takes some money out of her pocket.
A lot of money.

Billy   What the fuck's this for?

Victoria   This is all the money I could take out the bank.
You have it.

Billy   Who says I . . .

Victoria   I'm not worth much, Billy.
Just this.
I want to give it to you.

Billy   How much is there?

Victoria   A few thousand, I think.
It's for you. I got it for you.

Billy   Don't take the piss out of me.

Victoria   It's all I have.

She starts to take her clothes off.

Billy   You scare me, Vic.
The way you talk.
Dragging a body up a hill for you
and this . . .
My heart's thumping here.
I want you more than anything.
More than you can imagine.
You.
And you think I'm –
I'm – an employee.
Fuck yourself.

He starts to walk down the hill.

Victoria   Billy. Billy.
Wait.

He pauses.

He watches .
She takes the money, places it over **Oscar**'s *body.*
Pours petrol over it.

25

Norrie *standing.* **Annie** *returns.*

Annie   I've done it.

Norrie   OK. Stand back.

Norrie *exits.*

26

Victoria *throws the money on to the body.*
The sound of flames taking.
A fire.

Victoria   All I am.
On the fire.
Now I'm worthless.

Billy   You've thrown it away.
All that money. You're worth –
more.
More than that.

Victoria   Will you stay with me?

Billy   Course, Vic.

Victoria   We'll go to Spain together.
You knew him.
You should come.
We'll jump a train. Steal a car.
We'll work.
You have to come.

Billy   I'll come with you.

Victoria   It's the right thing, Billy.
It's right.

She takes the Co-op bag, with **Oscar***'s papers and book in it.*
She goes to put it on the fire.

Billy   You putting that on the fire?

Victoria   I read it.
Just history.

Billy   If that's what you want.

She puts it on the fire.

Victoria   It's what I want.
Like breaking through ice.
I'm breathing.

Billy *and* **Victoria**, *in the light of the flames.*

Old Victoria *enters.*
Carrying a small suitcase.
Goes to **Oscar**'s *grave.*

In the Red House.
Vicky *remembering.*

Victoria   Born here.

Old Victoria   Been over that water.
All the time I was away.
Thought about coming back.
Thought about how the place would hold me.
Shape of me in it.
Like a stone half in the ground.

Victoria   Come back.
And now all I want's to cross that water again.
Get away.

Vicky   Place's holding me.
Pulling me into it.

Old Victoria   Half in half out of the ground.

Vicky   Mountain, sea and forest.
Time before me and time after.

Victoria   Do you see me, Billy?

Billy   I see you fine.

Victoria   This is what I look like.
This is what the world looks like.

Vicky   Soft ground.
No lights.
Cold.
I recognise it.

Victoria   This is what it looks like.
After the fire.

Methuen Modern Plays
include work by

Jean Anouilh
John Arden
Margaretta D'Arcy
Peter Barnes
Sebastian Barry
Brendan Behan
Dermot Bolger
Edward Bond
Bertolt Brecht
Howard Brenton
Anthony Burgess
Simon Burke
Jim Cartwright
Caryl Churchill
Noël Coward
Lucinda Coxon
Sarah Daniels
Nick Darke
Nick Dear
Shelagh Delaney
David Edgar
David Eldridge
Dario Fo
Michael Frayn
John Godber
Paul Godfrey
David Greig
John Guare
Peter Handke
David Harrower
Jonathan Harvey
Iain Heggie
Declan Hughes
Terry Johnson
Sarah Kane
Charlotte Keatley
Barrie Keeffe
Howard Korder

Robert Lepage
Stephen Lowe
Doug Lucie
Martin McDonagh
John McGrath
Terrence McNally
David Mamet
Patrick Marber
Arthur Miller
Mtwa, Ngema & Simon
Tom Murphy
Phyllis Nagy
Peter Nichols
Joseph O'Connor
Joe Orton
Louise Page
Joe Penhall
Luigi Pirandello
Stephen Poliakoff
Franca Rame
Mark Ravenhill
Philip Ridley
Reginald Rose
David Rudkin
Willy Russell
Jean-Paul Sartre
Sam Shepard
Wole Soyinka
Shelagh Stephenson
C. P. Taylor
Theatre de Complicite
Theatre Workshop
Sue Townsend
Judy Upton
Timberlake Wertenbaker
Roy Williams
Victoria Wood

Methuen Contemporary Dramatists
include

Peter Barnes (three volumes)
Sebastian Barry
Edward Bond (six volumes)
Howard Brenton
  (two volumes)
Richard Cameron
Jim Cartwright
Caryl Churchill (two volumes)
Sarah Daniels (two volumes)
Nick Darke
David Edgar (three volumes)
Ben Elton
Dario Fo (two volumes)
Michael Frayn (two volumes)
Paul Godfrey
John Guare
Peter Handke
Jonathan Harvey
Declan Hughes
Terry Johnson (two volumes)
Bernard-Marie Koltès
David Lan
Bryony Lavery
Doug Lucie
David Mamet (three volumes)

Martin McDonagh
Duncan McLean
Anthony Minghella
  (two volumes)
Tom Murphy (four volumes)
Phyllis Nagy
Anthony Nielsen
Philip Osment
Louise Page
Joe Penhall
Stephen Poliakoff
  (three volumes)
Christina Reid
Philip Ridley
Willy Russell
Ntozake Shange
Sam Shepard (two volumes)
Wole Soyinka (two volumes)
David Storey (three volumes)
Sue Townsend
Michel Vinaver (two volumes)
Michael Wilcox
David Wood (two volumes)
Victoria Wood

Methuen World Classics
include

Jean Anouilh (two volumes)
John Arden (two volumes)
Arden & D'Arcy
Brendan Behan
Aphra Behn
Bertolt Brecht (six volumes)
Büchner
Bulgakov
Calderón
Čapek
Anton Chekhov
Noël Coward (seven volumes)
Eduardo De Filippo
Max Frisch
John Galsworthy
Gogol
Gorky
Harley Granville Barker
  (two volumes)
Henrik Ibsen (six volumes)
Lorca (three volumes)

Marivaux
Mustapha Matura
David Mercer (two volumes)
Arthur Miller (five volumes)
Molière
Musset
Peter Nichols (two volumes)
Clifford Odets
Joe Orton
A. W. Pinero
Luigi Pirandello
Terence Rattigan
  (two volumes)
W. Somerset Maugham
  (two volumes)
August Strindberg
  (three volumes)
J. M. Synge
Ramón del Valle-Inclán
Frank Wedekind
Oscar Wilde

Methuen Classical Greek Dramatists

Aeschylus Plays: One
(Persians, Seven Against Thebes, Suppliants,
Prometheus Bound)

Aeschylus Plays: Two
(Oresteia: Agamemnon, Libation-Bearers, Eumenides)

Aristophanes Plays: One
(Acharnians, Knights, Peace, Lysistrata)

Aristophanes Plays: Two
(Wasps, Clouds, Birds, Festival Time, Frogs)

Aristophanes & Menander: New Comedy
(Women in Power, Wealth, The Malcontent,
The Woman from Samos)

Euripides Plays: One
(Medea, The Phoenician Women, Bacchae)

Euripides Plays: Two
(Hecuba, The Women of Troy, Iphigeneia at Aulis,
Cyclops)

Euripides Plays: Three
(Alkestis, Helen, Ion)

Euripides Plays: Four
(Elektra, Orestes, Iphigeneia in Tauris)

Euripides Plays: Five
(Andromache, Herakles' Children, Herakles)

Euripides Plays: Six
(Hippolytos, Suppliants, Rhesos)

Sophocles Plays: One
(Oedipus the King, Oedipus at Colonus, Antigone)

Sophocles Plays: Two
(Ajax, Women of Trachis, Electra, Philoctetes)

Methuen Student Editions